Oscar Wilde

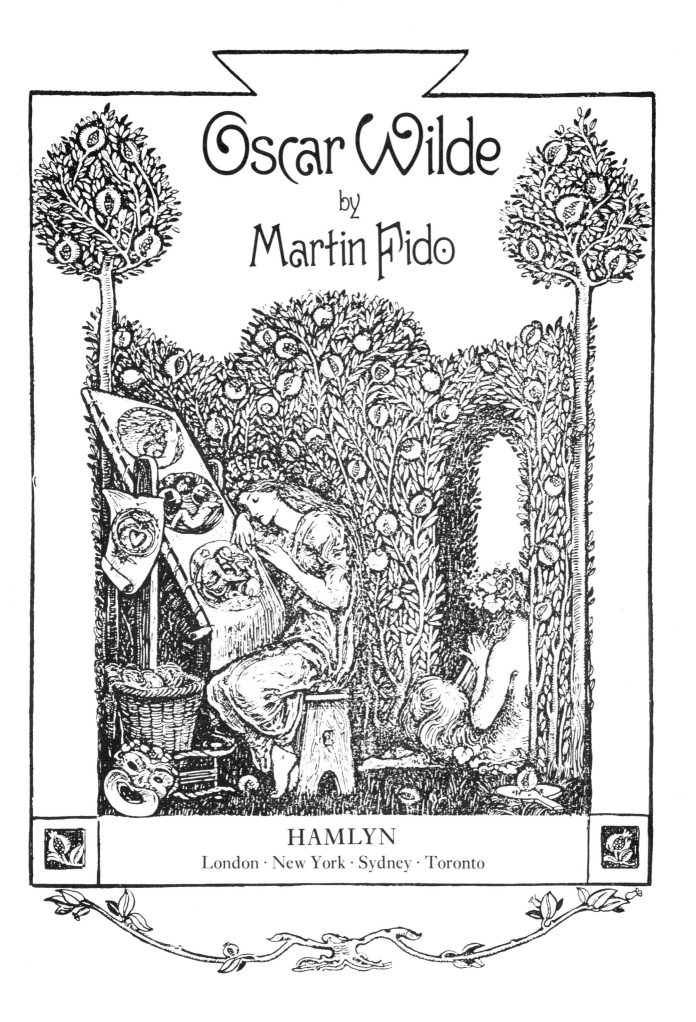

Oscar Wilde

by

Martin Fido

HAMLYN

London · New York · Sydney · Toronto

To Judith

Published by
The Hamlyn Publishing Group Limited
London · New York · Sydney · Toronto
Astronaut House, Feltham
Middlesex, England

© Copyright
The Hamlyn Publishing Group Limited 1973

Reprinted (twice) 1984

ISBN 0 600 36714 2

Text set in 'Monophoto' Ehrhardt
by London Filmsetters Limited

Printed in Yugoslavia

COLOUR PLATES

frontispiece
Oscar Wilde at the height of his fame. This photograph was
taken in 1895, just before the libel action against the Marquess
of Queensberry.

title page
The title page illustration from *A House of Pomegranates*, 1891.

CONTENTS

LEGEND and MAN of LETTERS

'I shall now live as the Infamous St. Oscar of Oxford, Poet and Martyr.'

Oscar Wilde is probably remembered first and foremost as a great, almost legendary, victim. He was savagely punished for a purely private weakness, which was itself unmentionable for fifty years after his death. 'Mummy, what did Oscar Wilde *do?*' was an unanswered question for several generations of precocious children, and evasion created mystery and myth. The unspoken came to be seen as the central fact, and for half a century Oscar Wilde reigned supreme as the foremost homosexual in the English mind. E. M. Forster's fictional hero Maurice could only describe himself as 'an unspeakable of the Oscar Wilde sort' when he recognised his own nature.

A common misapprehension today is that Wilde's conviction was an instance of peculiarly Victorian prudery and hypocrisy; that the first widely publicized case heard under the law that is now remembered as 'the blackmailer's charter' was a case for its time alone; that we could not have gaoled Oscar Wilde nowadays. This is untrue. The majority of Wilde's partner's were under the age of twenty-one, and the law today still refuses to the homosexual that freedom it allows to the heterosexual. In 1973, as in 1895, Oscar Wilde could have been imprisoned for adventures which, if undertaken with pretty girls, might have won him a certain coarse admiration from some policemen and lawyers.

Perhaps the most important myth to arise from the public exposure of Oscar Wilde was the belief that his personal style itself derived from his homosexuality. Shortly after his conviction, men with long hair were liable to have 'Oscar!' shouted derisively at them in the streets. Artistic sensibility could be regarded as a mark of effeminacy. Wit and elegance, articulacy and open charm, became suspect among men who wished to be noted for their virility. The late nineteenth century movement away from colour in men's clothes took fresh impetus from the exposed 'unmanliness' of a leading dandy. Yet Oscar Wilde's personal style had been adopted long before

his private life became exclusively homosexual – he was, after all, a married man with two children. And earlier history is filled with flamboyant, sensitive, long-haired men whose voracious heterosexuality was established beyond question. The cavalier poets, whose costume Wilde loved, are a good example.

Yet while the general public eschewed Wildean manners, there remained circles which affected them because they admired his example. In Oxford, studied indolence, supercilious elegance, and sartorial individualism were for years expected to mask the intellectual brilliance which might win academic honours without effort. Homosexuality itself had its periods of high fashion in the older universities, although Wilde himself had been neither conspicuously idle nor flagrantly gay as an undergraduate. But he left behind him a reputation which served as a model for later generations of students, and his histrionic style of life has been imitated and enjoyed by numerous young men who recognised the advantages accruing from early self-advertisement, although they have not necessarily shared Wilde's sexual or artistic tastes.

If Britain sees Wilde as a phantom of flagrant flamboyancy, his reputation abroad is more sternly intellectual. *Salome* and *De Profundis* were the works that won him fame in Germany. In the latter, Wilde summed up his literary position rather well. 'I was a man', he said, 'who stood in symbolic relation to the art and culture of my age.' He was not really one of the leading poets or thinkers of his age. His best plays were a refinement of the purely commercial theatre of the day, rather than conscious art. He discovered no major new talents in painting or poetry. He devised no literary techniques that greater men could use to greater effect (except perhaps for the use of witty stage dialogue, which Shaw transformed by applying it to far more serious ends). His theoretical aesthetic criticism was vitiated by an almost total ignorance of music, which he nonetheless proposed as the 'purest' art. His flashy references to Dvorak and private preference for Chopin reveal an ignorance of

Oscar Wilde, the self-conscious aesthete, with flowing tie, velvet coat, and the great fur-lined overcoat he bought for his visit to America.

Debussy which seriously weakens his posture as the intellectual impresario of *fin-de-siècle* art, and exposes the conservative tastes lying behind his public championing of the *avant-garde*. His reviewing was weakened by excessive generosity. His consciously exotic, decadent and 'Byzantine' poetry and drama now seems stiff, inert, and even tasteless, by virtue of his hackneyed overwriting. Yet for all this, the symbolic relation between the man and the art of the day was really there.

It was there in the public mind. When people thought of a representative poet, Aesthete, or generally artistic man, they were as likely as not to think of Wilde. His loud advertisement of ideas he received from Pater, Ruskin and Whistler associated him clearly with theoretical Aestheticism. His publication of poems and plays, no matter how mediocre, justified his claim to be an artist. And, no matter how uncertain his taste at times, his insistence upon allowing the latest theories of form and colour to influence his clothing and the decoration of his rooms made him a living example of the effect of art upon daily life.

Why, then, did this comparatively serious minor figure, the determined, if uneven, representative of his age's art and culture, become completely submerged in the British mind by the figure of the fallen pervert? Partly because the art which Wilde symbolised grew to no full flowering in Britain. Realism, a mode which Wilde and his associates regarded as the antithesis of art (although Wilde himself had the intelligence and taste to appreciate Ibsen) prevailed in English literature. Mannered writing forfeited critical esteem. A writer as artificial and aesthetic in his style as James Joyce would strike Home Secretaries and self-appointed censors more by the supposedly sordid nature of his matter than by the laboured perfection of his manner. In the visual arts, British Art Nouveau never recovered from the untimely death of Aubrey Beardsley. The whole movement Wilde had stood for perished from disregard in England, whereas on the continent it moved steadily through Dadaism and Surrealism to exert a continuing influence on living culture. And so Oscar Wilde holds a place of some distinction in German and French critical thought, while British critics are likely to dismiss him as a vapid dilettante pointing affectedly down a dead end.

Another reason for England's obsession with the legendary scandal is guilty fascination. Macaulay, writing of Byron, suggested that we have our public 'fits of morality' once every seven years or so. And he added that we make a horrid spectacle of ourselves: 'the savage envy of aspiring dunces... gratified by the agonies' of superior spirits and famous names, was his castigation. Byron endured this a hundred and fifty years ago. Oscar Wilde suffered eighty years ago. But the 'periodical fits of morality' continue, and they remain highly unedifying. As they proceed, we all enjoy the revelation of ever more salacious details. We are excited by the tension as we watch the unhappily eminent victim struggling to escape. We experience a certain elation, crowned by unimaginative moral self-satisfaction when he is finally disgraced, and our vehement indignation can be poured freely over him. Very, very few of us emerge with any credit at such times, and Britain's scandalous public 'affairs' are truly a grave indictment of your cruel curiosity and mine, rather than evidence of hypocrisy at the top of society.

And as we continue the nasty cultural habit, we remain fascinated by our ancestors' similar behaviour. We can enjoy the spectacle of a similar national orgasmic release being afforded to our grandparents, and share their erroneous impression that we are all better for yet another ritual self-pollution of society. Or alternatively, we can look at the public cruelty of the past and deceive ourselves into thinking that *they* were worse than we: *they* were meaninglessly brutal to weak men, whereas *we* have merely overplayed some justified public outrage.

Yet the fall of Oscar Wilde invites our attention for a more respectable reason than the gratification of lascivious smugness. He spoke truly when he said that he had put his genius into his life, and only his talent into his works. He unconsciously created in his life a perfect classical tragedy. He rose through qualities that were to bring him down, and the greatest of these was *hubris* – the overweening pride that challenges fate with fatuous self-confidence. Through arrogance, impudence, and impertinence, all beautifully restrained by his great qualities of kindness, gentleness, and sympathy, Wilde rose. When he reached the top he was the sweetest and most thoughtful of friends; the generous mentor of younger men; the most tolerant and forgiving of victims; the wittiest conversationalist and most engaging companion who ever lived. To his intimates he was a truly lovable man.

But for the world at large he adopted a different mask. He was haughty, supercilious, contemptuous, and indifferent to the feelings of mankind. He pleased himself, regardless of the fact that his vices might offend others who were more timorous or self-disciplined in their pleasure. His increasing obesity and occasional public drunkenness disgusted those who had to see him without knowing him. Because he sheathed his wit in tact to avoid hurting individuals, Oscar Wilde could not believe that people he had never met would be hurt by superior gibes hurled at

right In 'The Peacock Skirt', a decoration for the published version of Wilde's *Salome*, Aubrey Beardsley hit off the flowing lines, loose drapery, and peacock motif characteristic of the art and fashions with which Wilde identified himself.

below When people thought of an aesthete or a poet in the later nineteenth century they usually had someone like Oscar Wilde in mind. But it was not until after his trial that the successful self-advertisement of his younger days led them to mistakenly equate such an appearance with homosexuality. This American music sheet of the 1880s was a send-up of aestheticism, nothing else.

the tastes and attitudes of their class or nation. Because he was himself the first to forgive an enemy, and was totally incapable of kicking a man when he was down, he did not think it mattered if he raised up bitter enemies against himself, and could never have imagined that thousands of his nameless contemporaries were only waiting to have him at the mercy of their spite.

And so, with head held high, he contributed to his own downfall, and forced his life into the parabolic shape which remains his greatest artistic creation: The Tragedy of Oscar Wilde.

9

PRELUDE

'The happiness of a married man, my dear Gerald, depends on the people he has not married.'

Sir William Wilde, Surgeon-Oculist-in-Ordinary to Her Majesty, Fellow of the Royal College of Surgeons, Fellow of the Royal Irish Academy, Fellow of the Dublin Society, Member of the British Association, Member of the (Swedish) Order of the Polar Star, was a notoriously dirty old man. His personal uncleanliness was one of the jokes of Dublin. 'Why are Dr. Wilde's nails black?' asked his medical students, and answered themselves, 'Because he scratches himself.' His private life was equally well-known. According to popular opinion he was a man with 'a bastard in every farm-house'. Dr Henry Wilson, his medical partner, was in fact his natural son, and he had at least two other illegitimate children. Still, if Wilde was irresponsible about casual conception, he was responsible about the upbringing of his progeny. No one ever accused Sir William of leaving his bastards to starve. It was he who paid for Wilson's education and medical training, and gave him his position in Dublin society. His two illegitimate daughters were accepted members of the household of his clerical brother, the Reverend Ralph Wilde. Personal eccentricity was tolerated by easy-going Dublin society, and Sir William was known among his intimates as a good drinking companion.

He was also a man of outstanding and diverse abilities. Although he was never called upon to treat the royal family, his appointment as Surgeon-Oculist-in-Ordinary – a post created in his honour – was simply recognition of the fact that he was the best ear and eye-doctor in the British Isles, with a deserved reputation throughout Europe. He possessed the true courage and compassion of a great physician. As a seventeen-year-old student called back to his village home in Connaught to escape an outbreak of cholera in Dublin, he had diagnosed an unsuspected case of the disease in a local peasant, and then singlehanded nursed this patient whom the whole locality shunned, buried him when he died,

William Wilde, the brilliant young doctor Jane Francesca Elgee married. Engraving by T. H. Maguire, 1847.

Jane Francesca Wilde at the height of her success as a Dublin hostess.

and fumigated his hovel, thus saving the villagers from the epidemic that their terrified inaction might have brought upon them. As a young doctor travelling in Egypt he had come into contact with widespread trachoma, and proceeded to study ophthalmology at Moorfields and Vienna. When he began to practise in Dublin, he freely offered his services to the poor, and the reputation he established among them as a man who could make the blind see and the deaf hear spread to the upper classes, who soon gave Dr William Wilde a lucrative fashionable practice.

At the same time he was building a reputation as a generally learned man. He had examined the magnificent archaeological remains of Egypt, and continued to take an interest in archaeology on his return to Ireland. He became a leading authority on his country's early history. He wrote travel books after his journeys abroad, and these enjoyed considerable success. His book on Austria was strengthened by precise and well-ordered statistical information, which was noted by the government. Wilde was appointed Medical Census Commissioner, and provided accurate, well-tabulated and moving factual evidence of the effects of the terrible potato-blight of the 1840s. The Royal Irish Academy turned to him to compile a descriptive catalogue of their collection of Irish antiquities – a task which had driven a committee to despair before Wilde completed it alone. When he was created a Knight of St Patrick in 1864, the Viceroy observed that his professional skill already enjoyed European recognition; the knighthood was to honour 'the distinguished services you have rendered to statistical science'.

1864 saw Sir William Wilde at the peak of his career. He was much in demand as a lecturer to learned societies and contributor to learned journals. He had prospered, and now lived in the spacious Georgian townhouse, No. 1 Merrion Square, at the heart of fashionable Dublin. He owned two country retreats: a fishing lodge at Illaunroe, on Lough Fee, Galway, and a villa he had built at Moytura, overlooking Lough Corrib. He enjoyed an international reputation, and numbered among his friends the ablest and most learned men of Ireland. His deplorable scruffiness and sociable love of the bottle could be overlooked as quaint personal foibles. As for his womanising, his wife could rise above paying it any attention, so why should anyone else care?

Lady Wilde towered over her husband physically. Her hands and feet were disproportionately large on what was already a body of Junoesque proportions. Her strong aquiline features were more handsome than beautiful. The size of her bottom drew

attention, but the majesty of her presence ensured that she never seemed clumsy or awkward. Mundane matters were beneath her consideration. She allowed her house to become almost as dirty and untidy as her husband. 'Why do you put the plates on the coal-scuttle?' she asked her servant. 'What are the chairs made for?' For she was, in her own estimation, 'the acknowledged voice in poetry of all Ireland'.

When Jane Francesca Elgee was about twenty she saw a large crowd gathered for the funeral of a man whose name she had never heard. When she asked who he was, she was told, simply, 'A poet.' Her ambition was immediately fired. A young poet, apparently, was accorded public esteem. She discovered that the dead man had contributed patriotic verses to the nationalist journal *The Nation*. Obviously he had left a gap to be filled, and soon verse translations over the name of Speranza, and patriotic letters over the name of John Fanshawe Ellis began to appear in *The Nation*. These contributions reached the newspaper office as 'little scented notes, sealed with wax of a delicate hue and dainty device', and they intrigued the editor, Gavan Duffy. But Mr Ellis refused his invitations to call at the office, and was only with difficulty persuaded to receive Duffy at a house in Leeson Street. Duffy was romantically delighted when his new contributor turned out to be 'a tall girl . . . whose stately carriage and figure, flashing brown eyes, and features cast in a heroic mould, seemed fit for the genius of poetry, or the spirit of revolution'.

Jane Elgee, the obscure grand-daughter of a Church of Ireland archdeacon, was metamorphosed into Speranza, the Young Ireland nationalist and poetess.

Her poetry was consistently dreadful. She maintained a tone of unslackening stridency and mixed dead metaphors with gay abandon. Her metrical ear was lamentably deficient. When she tried to follow Tennyson's *Locksley Hall* metre she managed to leave an awkward pause in place of a syllable in her very first line:

Vain the love that looketh upward,
   we may worship,   adore:
From the heart's o'erflowing chalice
   all the tide of feeling pour.

When she invented her own metre to celebrate the patriotism of one of her Young Ireland friends, she produced an inglorious bouncing combination of trochees and anapests rather like an abbreviated and reversed poulterer's measure:

Thus in glory is he seen,
   tho' his years are yet but green,

One anointed as head of our nation:
For high Heaven hath decreed that a soul
   like this must lead,
Let us kneel, then, in deep adoration.

But she was a public personality, and when in 1848 she wrote a leader for *The Nation* urging the Irish to rise in support of Smith O'Brien's abortive rebellion, the government cautiously decided that her youth and sex would make it imprudent to prosecute her for treason. Duffy, as editor, was tried instead, but Speranza created a sensation at the trial by standing up in the body of the court and declaring her own responsibility for the piece.

Somewhere around this time Speranza met William Wilde. Dublin gossip had it that they were lovers before their marriage in 1851. Speranza gently withdrew from political activity, and accepted the congenial role of hostess to Dublin's celebrities and wife to the thirty-six year old doctor. They were an odd, but not ill-matched couple. Both were intelligent and published books; both were at once concerned for the distresses of the Irish poor, and yet snobbishly delighted by the English aristocracy of the vice-regal court. Her artistic and poetic inclinations happily complemented his scientific and archaeological learning. He knew great men, like the brilliant mathematician, Sir William Rowan Hamilton, as intimates. She could offer them feminine sympathy and the setting of her salon in which to bask. They rose together from respectable Westland Row to fashionable Merrion Square; from brilliant youth to distinguished middle age; from Dr Wilde and Speranza to Sir William and Lady Wilde. 1864 was their year of triumph and

disaster: the year of the knighthood and the year of Mary Josephine Travers.

She was the unmarried twenty-nine year old daughter of the Professor of Medical Jurisprudence at Trinity College. Ten years earlier she had been sent to Wilde to have treatment for an inflammation of the ear. Wilde had taken a fatherly interest in her; lent her books; taken her to public lectures; entertained her in his home; and, at last, found that his interest was no longer as fatherly as it had been. Mary Josephine, unfortunately, was an unbalanced and hysterical girl. She accepted Wilde's sympathy and attentions, and slipped easily into the casual Bohemian life of No. 1 Merrion Square. She allowed the doctor to buy clothes for her, and borrowed money from him. Occasionally she offered postage stamps in repayment. By 1861 this beautiful friendship was becoming an embarrassment to Wilde. He suspected that Speranza was following him and Mary Josephine around Dublin to spy on them.

Mary was accosted by Speranza in the study of the Merrion Square house. 'Do you want to take my husband away from me?' she asked cheerfully. But she accompanied the light pleasantry with a painful pinch. Mary Josephine proved impervious to hints.

She sent Wilde a photograph he had earlier requested, accompanying it with a letter criticising Speranza's grandly insulting manner. Wilde, by now anxious to be free of the entanglement, let Speranza send a chilling reply:

Dear Miss Travers,
   Dr Wilde returns your photograph.
     Yours very truly,
      Jane Wilde

The break came when Mary Josephine walked, uninvited, into Speranza's bedroom. She was firmly and finally put out of the house.

From then on, Mary Josephine envinced a maniacal hatred of both Wildes. William told his wife that the girl was mad, and in the light of her subsequent conduct this may well have been a considered and accurate diagnosis, as well as a convenient story. Mary Josephine began a campaign of persecution by anonymous letters. Pseudonymous letters to the press attacked Wilde, and angry letters to the house called him a 'spiteful old lunatic'. She went to the length of having cards printed, announcing her own death, and sent them to Speranza.

Wilde tried desperately to buy her off. He offered her reasonable sums of money. He leaped at her suggestion that she might go to Australia, and gave her money for her passage. She changed her mind, and spent the money. When she next proposed Australia, Wilde offered to accompany her to the ship. They got as far as Liverpool before she changed her mind again.

The accolade of 1864 finally drove Mary Josephine to new heights of demented activity. She published a pamphlet, assuming for the purpose Lady Wilde's famous pseudonym, Speranza, in which she described the rape of one 'Florence Boyle Price' by a 'Dr Quilp'. When newsboys were hired to distribute this scurrilous story outside a hall where Sir William was lecturing on 'Ireland, Past and Present', no one doubted that it was he who was accused of violating a patient after overcoming her with chloroform.

Lady Wilde took her children on holiday to Bray to escape the persecution, but Miss Travers followed and sent newsboys to the door of her house to hand in pamphlets. Finally Lady Wilde wrote in her loftiest tone to Dr Travers, informing him of his daughter's 'disreputable conduct . . . at Bray, where she consorts with all the newspaper boys in the place . . . and . . . makes it appear that she has had an intrigue with Sir William Wilde'. It was Mary Josephine's opportunity, and she seized it gladly. Finding the letter among her father's papers, she took it directly to her solicitors, and started a libel action against the Wildes.

The situation was absurd. For weeks Mary Josephine had been publishing unquestionable libels on Sir William Wilde, maliciously calculated to bring him into 'hatred and contempt': now she was able to force him into court as a co-defendant, since as a husband he was legally responsible for his wife's trivial offence of writing a single unflattering description of Mary Josephine to a single third party.

Court-room publicity was all Mary Josephine really asked. She had no qualms about publishing

left An illustration of the Cong River from Sir William Wilde's book, *Lough Corrib*.

below No. 1 Merrion Square, Oscar Wilde's boyhood home in the heart of fashionable Dublin.

above left Charles Gavan Duffy, the editor of *The Nation*.
Seeking the acquaintance of 'Mr Ellis' he met instead Miss
Elgee, who was to become known as Speranza.

top Speranza, 'The acknowledged voice of poetry in all Ireland',
was also the proud and handsome Lady Wilde; her son Oscar
admired and adored her. From a drawing by Morosini.

left Sir William Wilde, wearing his Swedish Order of the Pole
Star, and displaying all his notorious scruffiness. Not only does
he look as though he has been sleeping in his court dress, he
seems blissfully unaware that the camera is recording his
missing button.

above Dr. Henry Wilson, illegitimate son of Sir William Wilde.
The half-brother who tried to compel Oscar to remain
Protestant by threatening to will away their joint inheritance
from their father.

her own shame to the world, as long as the lover who had discarded her and the superior wife who had despised her might be humiliated in the witness-box.

The case provided a great opportunity for Irish forensic eloquence. Mary Josephine's counsel gave a moving description of his client's loss of honour at the hands of a man old enough to be her father, and bound by his professional duty to respect her person. The plaintiff herself told a strange new story. Chloroform was no longer responsible for her helpless condition: now she claimed that Sir William's strong hands had choked her until she passed out, and when she recovered her senses she realized that the medical fiend had ravished her prostrate body.

Cross-examination dented this melodramatic tale. It seemed that the virtuous young lady had been curiously willing to continue visiting her molester. She had made no complaint about the rape at the time, and had instead accepted presents of clothes and money from Dr Wilde. She denied that she had continued to be his mistress, but even by her own account had been practising something unpleasantly like blackmail.

Speranza elicited some sympathy by her dignity and loyalty to her husband when she stood in the witness-box. But nobody believed her firm denial that anything improper had taken place between Sir William and Miss Travers, and her attitude of lofty superiority to any allegations of immorality created an unfavourable impression on a public which held that ladies should be shockable.

It was Sir William's failure to go into the box and deny Mary Josephine's charges that created the worst impression. Saying nothing suggested that he must have something to hide. And allowing his wife to speak for him suggested a lack of moral courage. Legally his decision not to give evidence may have been perfectly proper, but it did more than anything else to damage his reputation. The jury found that Speranza had libelled Mary Josephine, but awarded only a farthing damages, that being, in their view, the derisory value of the young lady's honour. But the Wildes had to pay costs, and their social standing was subtly altered. Hitherto they had been an odd couple: now they were a sinister couple. Speranza had appeared too proud to act sensibly in a matter that concerned her closely, and had given an impression that she held a Bohemian contempt for the middle-class moral decencies. Sir William was seen, at best, as a lascivious coward who hid behind his wife's skirts rather than face cross-examination himself. At worst he was suspected of having actually raped a patient, and thereby fulfilled one of the deep fears of Victorian society.

At the time all this took place Oscar Wilde was ten. He seems to have known little of the affair, and never doubted that his parents' name was unsmirched. But Sir William Wilde's downfall provided an aesthetically perfect overture to his son's more terrible collapse. The main theme of each was scandal, and each was played out in a court-room. Both Wildes suffered as a consequence of libel actions: both fell from their points of highest achievement. Like his mother, Oscar was to create a favourable impression on some auditors and jurors by his courage and determination, yet would offend more by his casual disregard for truth and conventional moral sensitivity. And one lesson which the family felt had been learned from the earlier case was to have terrible repercussions when applied to the later. Sir William had failed to face the music: Oscar was not to feel free to run away.

Sir William and Lady Wilde, caricatured by Harry Furniss.

AN IRISH UPBRINGING

'I do not approve of anything that tampers with natural ignorance. Ignorance is like a delicate exotic fruit; touch it and the bloom is gone. The whole theory of modern education is radically unsound. Fortunately in England, at any rate, education produces no effect whatsoever. If it did, it would prove a serious danger to the upper classes.'

Oscar Wilde was born on 16 October 1854, at No. 21 Westland Row, Dublin. Two years earlier his elder brother Willie had received all the necessary family names: William for his father, Charles for Speranza's father, Kingsbury for Speranza's mother's family, and Wills for Sir William's best-established connections. At Oscar's christening Speranza was free to indulge her poetic and nationalistic ardour. He was given two names from the ancient literature of Ireland: Oscar and Fingal. The name O'Flahertie celebrated the heroic family which dominated the history of Sir William's west coast home. Wills was not entered on his birth certificate, although Oscar sometimes used the name in later life.

It was said that Speranza had hoped for a daughter. This may well be true, as she already had one son. It was said that Speranza dressed Oscar in girl's clothes. This is true in a way: all middle-class Victorian boys were dressed in petticoats during their infancy. Oscar's sister Isola was not born until he was three, at which time he would still have been wearing skirts, no matter how much his mother wished to develop his virility. It was said that Speranza treated Oscar as a girl for a long time. But this seems to be nothing but scandalous invention after the event, seeking a simple explanation for Wilde's homosexuality. Isola satisfied Speranza's need for a daughter, and the poetess who had given her son extravagantly heroic bardic names was hardly likely to wish to make a woman of him.

But if it is absurd to believe that Speranza consciously trained her son in effeminacy, it is only just to observe that the personalities of the Wilde parents combined to provide exactly the psychological environment most conducive to uncertain sexual identity in their offspring. When the family moved to Merrion Square in 1856, Speranza came to dominate home life increasingly. The new large house was better fitted for her salon, and the Dublin press described her in flattering terms as a leading hostess. Sir William, on the other hand, was within easy walking distance of his hospital, and met his preferred social circle at work, or in taverns. The children were frequently taken on holiday to Sandymount or Bray by their mother: Sir William rarely came too. Even before the Mary Travers scandal, Sir William had begun to spend as much time as possible in the west. His villa at Moytura gave him great pleasure as it was within reach of the sites at which he performed the fine archaeological work of the last years of his life. During his impressionable childhood years, then, Oscar had a father whose presence was never certain, and whose personality was retiring. His mother, on the other hand, was impressive to the point of seeming overwhelming. Speranza's clothes grew increasingly striking and eccentric. She fashioned poetic robes capped by a wreath of laurels for herself, in which to greet her salon. Her self-assurance grew, and with it her lordly and commanding presence. She set the tone of the household, in which the curtains might be drawn by day, so that visitors could only see her under flattering pink candlelight.

Psychoanalysts argue that the growing mind unconsciously perceives the differences between the sexes as presented by parents, and moulds its own attitudes in accordance with their observed gender-determined behaviour. In circumstances like those in the Wilde household, the child may refuse to identify himself with the weaker parental model. If there is nothing particularly attractive about the father-figure, whereas the mother-figure seems splendid, the male child *may* (which is not to say *will*) unconsciously identify himself with his mother and incorporate into his personality a number of feminine attitudes, including, ultimately, sexual attraction to men rather than women. If such a reading of the

psychopathology of the homosexual is correct, then there is no cause for surprise in Wilde's later career: his 'unnatural' sexual development was, in fact, perfectly natural.

In other respects the Wildes were extremely good parents, and Oscar showed himself their child in some attractive ways. They were a brilliant couple, and Oscar was fortunate in inheriting scholarly aptitude from his father at the same time as he more

right Oscar Wilde's birthplace in Westland Row, Dublin.

below 'Botany Bay', Trinity College, Dublin. The quadrangle where Wilde had rooms as a student.

obviously developed his mother's literary sensibility. A generous, but never painful or strident, social conscience was inculcated by the example of the Wilde parents. In adult life Oscar Wilde was to show a remarkable capacity to write and converse sympathetically on behalf of Russian Nihilism, Irish Nationalism, and European Socialism, without ever losing his foothold in fashionable high bourgeois and minor aristocratic drawing-rooms. Personal kindness was practised and learned in the home at Merrion Square, and family loyalty was always a marked feature of the Wildes' life. Even when Willie Wilde had grown up to become a rather vulgar alcoholic journalist who was not easy for Oscar to tolerate, overt criticism of his brother was one way to lose Oscar's friendship.

On the debit side Oscar inherited his parents' love of titled society and was fairly undisguisedly a snob. More dangerously, Sir William's vacillating inactivity when brought up against the consequences of his actions could be observed in his son at the time of the latter's final crisis. And from Speranza he adopted a manner of lofty superiority which would win him many enemies, and a disregard for truth which would prove disastrous in the witness-box.

Less dangerously, Speranza cultivated his tastes and attitudes. Eccentric clothing never perturbed Oscar, and flamboyant personal ornamentation became a habit. He grew to love jewelled rings and jewelled prose. Speranza encouraged her son to value the highly artificial novels of Bulwer Lytton and Disraeli above plainer and greater works of Victorian fiction. Her uncle Charles Maturin's Gothic romance *Melmoth the Wanderer* was a book that mother and son both held to be one of the major works of the early nineteenth century.

Surprisingly, for so sophisticated and cosmopolitan a man, Oscar Wilde derived from his mother a lifelong willingness to accept superstitions. One of the few incidents recalled from his childhood has him waking up at night, crying, and asking, 'Why are they beating that dog?' He was soothed and assured that no one was beating a dog, but the next day it was found that one of his relatives had died, and for the rest of his life Oscar believed that he had heard the banshee which wails for the spirits of the departing in Ireland.

In 1864 Oscar was sent away to Portora Royal School with his brother Willie. The Royal schools of Ulster and Leinster were founded in the seventeenth century to reinforce England's Protestant ascendancy over Ireland. Occasional commissions of enquiry had subsequently discovered that they tended to accept public funds and endowments without necessarily accepting any pupils to give actual employment to the comfortably reimbursed

right The honours board in the Steele Hall, Portora. Oscar Wilde's name was, apparently, missing from the board for some time after the trial; when it was restored the letters were painted a little larger.

far right Portora's distinguished alumnus, restored to the honours board, is also represented by this portrait.

below The child Oscar, wearing a blue velvet dress.

below right The main school building at Portora Royal School, as it was when Wilde was a schoolboy.

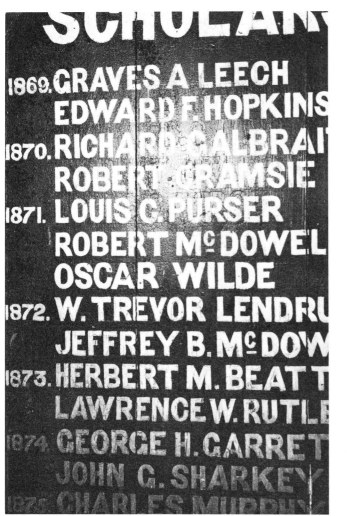

Dublin in the second half of the 19th century. 'The
city of dreadful knights', Oscar later called it,
though he was really very proud of his father's title
and professional distinction.

masters. But Portora had emerged well from these disquieting investigations, and the worst that could be said of it in the 1860s was that it accepted a disproportionately high number of boys from upper class families, and virtually no Catholics. In fact, it was simply a good public school of the period, under the direction of the Church of Ireland, and the appropriate place for a leading Dublin doctor to send his son.

Willie Wilde was a more successful public schoolboy than Oscar. Bluff, hearty and athletic he fought his way into school favour, while his unathletic younger brother had less to offer a world of boys. Oscar occasionally took a boat out on Lake Erne, although he was noted as a poor oarsman. He was given the mysterious nickname of 'Grey-crow', from an island on the lake, and this apparently annoyed him greatly.

After Oscar had been three years at Portora, his little sister Isola died while staying with an uncle in Edgeworthstown. Oscar was deeply distressed, and the local doctor, who watched him paying long and frequent visits to her grave, felt that he seemed inconsolable.

Four years later, although he may not have known it, Oscar lost two more sisters. Emily and Mary, the illegitimate children who lived with the Reverend Ralph Wilde, were burned to death in an accident at a ball in Drumsnatt. They were still in their early twenties, and the terrible tragedy increased Sir William's tendency to retreat from Dublin social life to the calm and peace of Moytura.

A month before this, Oscar had started his undergraduate career at Trinity College, Dublin. After a slow start he had proved himself a fine classical scholar at Portora, and he left the school with a gold medal for classics, and a place on the honours boards. Within a few weeks of starting at Trinity he had been elected a Queen's Scholar, and over the next three years he was to win prizes for Greek verse and classics, and finally the Berkeley Gold Medal. A study of his surviving examination marks suggests that his abilities were too high for him ever to fall far below standards of academic excellence, but he was particularly likely to exert himself when prizes or a movement forward in his career were in the offing. He was helped by a quick and retentive memory.

The Reverend John Pentland Mahaffy, Precentor and Junior Dean of the College, was Wilde's tutor in Greek, and probably the earliest strong influence on him, after his mother. Mahaffy was one of the memorable Dublin characters: a first rate scholar, a conversationalist of even higher quality, and a clergyman of decidedly doubtful reverence. The pagan life of the ancient Greeks was Mahaffy's

right John Pentland Mahaffy, the most influential of Wilde's university tutors. From a painting by William Orpen.

below Trinity College, Dublin.

intellectual passion. Compared with that, the salvation by Christian grace he was supposed to profess seemed of limited interest and dubious value. He was a notorious anti-Catholic and freethinker, and a longstanding visitor to Speranza's salon. Socially he was a great diner-out and snob, and Wilde probably learned from him as much about the use of wit and flattery to win a safe place at aristocratic dinner-tables as he did about Greek civilisation.

Not that Mahaffy neglected his pupil's academic needs. He gave Wilde a confident mastery of Greek, and took him into his confidence about his own scholarly labours. When *Social Life in Greece from Homer to Menander* appeared, Mahaffy generously acknowledged help from the talented student, claiming that he had made 'improvements and corrections all through the book'. Such a tribute from a leading scholar was a real feather in Oscar Wilde's cap.

For all this academic success, he was not one of the notable undergraduates of his day at Trinity. Once again it was Willie who succeeded with bluff young Irish manhood. Willie drank and whored his way through college in a way his fellow students respected. On one notable occasion, Sir William Wilde chaired a Philosophical Society meeting at which Willie, to his father's thorough approval, delivered a resounding defence of the institution of prostitution. Both were in their element at such a bawdy, boozy gathering. Oscar, by contrast, despised his Irish student contemporaries, and later told a friend:

'They thought of nothing but running and jumping: they varied these intellectual exercises with bouts of fighting and drinking. If they had any souls, they diverted them with coarse amours among barmaids and the women of the streets. They were simply awful.'

There were few companions with the sensitivity to appreciate the landscape painting which stood upon an easel in his rooms in the part of the college known as Botany Bay. Oscar pretended that it was his own uncompleted work: 'I have just put in the butterfly,' he would say. To one friend he remarked, 'Come home with me. I want to introduce you to my mother. We have founded a society for the suppression of virtue.' Such quietly flippant cynicism was not really appreciated among the more broadly oafish Protestant youth of Trinity. Oscar's loyal supporters in Dublin were dons rather than students. When it transpired that Edward Carson, a Trinity undergraduate contemporary, was to appear against Oscar in the first of his disastrous trials, Oscar seems to have assumed, wrongly, that Carson would as a matter of course be personally prejudiced against him.

The Berkeley Gold Medal for Greek, awarded to Oscar Wilde by Trinity College in 1874. At difficult moments in Wilde's later life the medal sometimes found its way into pawnshops.

OXFORD

'It was admirable at Oxford, where the worst that could happen to you was a reprimand from the Dean or a lecture from the President, and where the highest excitement was Magdalen becoming head of the river, and the lighting of a bonfire in the quad as a celebration of the august event.'

Oscar Wilde left Trinity College with further academic honours. He won a demyship, or scholarship worth £95 a year for four years, to Magdalen College, Oxford. And in leaving Dublin for Oxford he left a happy, if somewhat unconventional, family life for a life of legend. The brilliant undergraduate, peacocking his way from his gaudily Aesthetic rooms to the road he helped build under John Ruskin's personal direction; the young wit, who floored bullying sportsmen with charming epigrams, even as they dragged his distastefully fastidious person up country hills; the fantastically dressed student poet, set a tone which became famous – or notorious – for generations in Oxford.

So that it is worth stressing that for at least two and a half of his four Oxford years, Wilde behaved like a perfectly normal undergraduate, distinguished by nothing more than the excellent intellect which gained him first-class honours in his public examinations. Existing photographs show that the great dandy dressed like any other well-to-do student of the 1870s, in vivid check suits. There was nothing particularly Aesthetic about the curly bowler he affected, and the unfortunate fact that he inherited from his mother a large, rather ungainly and ill-proportioned frame, meant that he looked more like a sporty bookmaker of the period than a hypersensitive poet.

Wilde's interests at this time were those of any other intelligent, sensitive young man. Oxford was still dizzy from the religious blows it had suffered in the 1830s and '40s, when its brilliant clerical dons had tried to drag the Church of England into a more historical and catholic posture but had lost their leader, John Henry Newman, to Rome, and after him a whole host of students and young people. The

university establishment of the 1870s was composed of men like Jowett of Balliol and Pattison of Lincoln who, in their younger days, had suffered agonies of conscience as they wondered whether to follow Newman. And the Catholic question – to convert or not to convert – remained the central intellectual issue for undergraduates, who were far too young and inexperienced to have formed any opinions about the newer Aesthetic and political ideas emanating from Pater and Ruskin until they had actually come under the influence of the two men. So for his first couple of years in Oxford, Oscar Wilde made no Aesthetic impression on a wondering town, but went through the flirtation with Rome that had been a conventional pattern for serious young men over the previous thirty years.

Sharing the spiritual struggle with him were a group of charming young Magdalen men, quite unlike the Hogarthian students of Dublin. 'Bouncer'

left Walter Pater, Fellow of Brasenose College, Oxford. His cult of the beautiful was enthusiastically adopted by the young Wilde, and he became one of the greatest admirers of Wilde's ornate prose tales.

right Oscar Wilde at the age of twenty.

Ward, 'Kitten' Harding, 'Dunskie' Hunter-Blair, were the lightly nicknamed friends with whom 'Hoskie' Wilde discussed the attractions of Papism and went to masses at the newly-built Jesuit church of St Aloysius. Their letters to each other in the vacations mingled Latin and Greek tags, student slang, youthful ebullience, and earnest doubt. Oscar spent a great deal of time playing lawn tennis, and spent his summers with rod and gun in the west of Ireland, catching 'Sea-Trout and Occasional Salmon', and shooting a lot of hares, but not many grouse. He was a strong swimmer and a good horseman, and very far indeed from the limp-wristed camping Aesthete of legend. Pretty girls escorted to church were something of which one might boast to friends: alternately, a very cautious query might be put as to what exactly a student known to them was doing with a choirboy, and whether it was wise for the man to associate with 'Bouncer' and 'Hoskie' if

he really was entangled with the lad. When a finished Aesthetic art-critic, Lord Ronald Sutherland-Gower, came down to Oxford with his friend Frank Miles to look over the students, he found Wilde's 'long-haired head full of nonsense regarding the Church of Rome. His room filled with photographs of the Pope and of Cardinal Manning'.

Not that scrupulous religiosity could ever have overwhelmed Oscar Wilde. At the very time when he was most fascinated by the Scarlet Woman his love of ritual also led him in a direction forbidden to Catholics, and he became an enthusiastic Freemason. Nor was he attracted by asceticism or celibacy. He loved the richness of Rome, and responded to beauty wherever he found it.

At home in the vacations he began to see much of a girl named Florence Balcombe. She was unusually beautiful, and he sketched her, and gave her a sketch of the view from Moytura. They exchanged small presents, culminating in Oscar's giving her a golden cross inscribed with his name. Florence was not well off, and the match would not have been a prudent one from the Wildes' point of view. But Oscar felt that some degree of serious commitment had been made. When, in the year he left Oxford, she married another young Irishman (who was to become famous as the creator of *Dracula*) he was put out, and asked for the return of his trinkets. His stiff manner implied that he had been slighted, if not jilted. Certainly he had lost something. The future Mrs Bram Stoker was, in the opinion of no less a judge than George du Maurier, one of the three or four most beautiful women of the time.

Altogether it would have seemed safe to predict a conventional career for the lively second-year undergraduate who startled his uncle, the Vicar of West Ashby, by sending long telegrams where most people would have sent postcards, yet who listened meekly to avuncular sermons that he accepted as a gentle reproof to himself. It seemed that Speranza's ecstatic admiration of her two sons would prove nothing but every mother's conviction that *her* geese really are the rarest of whooper swans. Willie looked set towards a modest career at the Dublin bar, and Oscar, provided he attained the First in Mods and Greats for which he was working, might reasonably hope for a college fellowship, and the quiet life of an able don.

The first blow to this peaceful middle-class idyll was the death of Sir William in April 1876. It immediately transpired that his affairs were in a state of quite unexpected disorder, and something would have to be done about supporting Speranza. Somehow, Sir William had secretly been squandering money for years. He left a mere £7,000, and thousands of pounds of debts. No one knew where his money had gone: Speranza was completely bewildered by a recent loan of £1,000 that had melted without her observing any unusual expenditure on her husband's part. All that was left from the comfortable Dublin practice was a handful of mortgaged buildings in Ireland. Willie inherited No. 1 Merrion Square, and Moytura, out of which he was expected to pay an annuity of £200 to his mother in addition to paying off mortgages standing on the properties. Oscar got some mortgaged houses at Bray, and shared the Illaunroe fishing-lodge with his half-brother Henry Wilson.

Illaunroe played an interesting part in Oscar's early manhood. He stayed in it himself, and took his artist friend Frank Miles with him on fishing holidays. He made arrangements to let it and thereby supplement his income. He almost lost it altogether when Wilson, who died a year after his father, tried

left below John Henry (later Cardinal) Newman. His Catholic influence on Oxford was considerable and he made a deep personal impression on Wilde. Chalk drawing by George Richmond.

right below The young John Ruskin. He became Slade Professor of Fine Art in 1869 and taught Wilde a great deal about the appreciation of pictures. His combination of idealistic socialism with aesthetics may also have influenced Wilde. Chalk drawing by George Richmond.

below George du Maurier, who drew cartoons of fashionable and artistic life for *Punch*. Oscar imitated the style du Maurier caricatured, and the quips of the one appeared as the captions of the other, and vice versa.

he proposing the day they met as fellow-travellers, and she breaking it off as soon as she reached home and realised that he was more interested in money than love.

Oscar's first duty was clearly to complete his degree and fulfil his splendid academic promise. Without seriously reducing his chances of doing well in his Finals, he did undoubtedly begin to assume some of the airs of a university character after he had successfully taken first-class honours in the interim exam, Mods. When 'Bouncer' Ward completed his degree and went down, Oscar took over his rooms in Magdalen's beautiful cloisters, and decorated them famously with a piano, lots of pictures, and two details that showed him aware at last of fashionable Aestheticism: a grey carpet, and a collection of blue and white Japanese china. The stairs in Magdalen cloisters are notoriously steep, and narrow awkwardly towards the foot, so that it is easy to believe that with little physical violence, Oscar was able to use a superior position to discomfort a gang of student hearties who came up with the intention of smashing his china. Later, in America, he told reporters that a sermon had been preached against him in the University Church for saying that he wished he could live up to his blue china. In this case, he either told the same story to George du Maurier, who used the line for a *Punch* cartoon, or perhaps borrowed du Maurier's line for a piece of fictitious self-advertisement. As Jimmy Whistler was to observe, it was hard to say whether du Maurier discovered Wilde or Wilde discovered du Maurier: so many epigrams were attributed to the one at the same time as they captioned the cartoons of the other.

Like all truly fashionable Oxford men, Wilde now came to realise that the highest reputation within the university was won by making some sort of name outside it. He began to spend more and more time in London, cultivating Lord Ronald Gower, and the aristocratic Aesthetic set to which he offered an entry. He improved his friendship with Frank Miles. He took a naively sophisticated delight in meeting titled ladies of dangerous reputation. He learned to use languid flippancy to mask social unease.

He also began to write. His parentage gave him a nodding acquaintance with the Dublin literary world, and he could get poems published in Ireland where another student might have failed. He used his position in England to offer Irish journals reviews of London art exhibitions, striking out early for that position as a general commentator on the arts which was, for years, to be more truly his rôle than his vocation of poet.

He used the classic device of young men who want to be noticed: he sent copies of his work, on one

The Sheldonian Theatre, Oxford, where Wilde gave a public reading of his poem *Ravenna*, which won him the Newdigate Prize.

to cut him out from inheriting the lodge on the grounds that Oscar was flirting with Rome. Oscar was furious at such bigotry, but swallowed his pride, and soft-pedalled his papistry until the lodge was securely his. Some time after he left Oxford he probably sold it.

The death of Sir William had more immediate consequences for Speranza and Willie than for Oscar. They had to arrange the sale of No. 1 Merrion Square, and move to cheaper accommodation in London. Speranza hoped that Willie's idleness as a law student might pay off. He had spent more time at the ice-rink than at his studies, but at least, his mother hoped, there should now be a wealthy marriage in prospect to save the family fortunes. Alas, for all the Wildes' concealment of their new poverty, Willie's intended got wind of it, and her parents broke off the match. Still, Willie was encouraged to continue wife-hunting until, about ten years later, he actually did marry a rich woman, having in the interim enjoyed a whirlwind engagement to the seventeen-year-old Ethel Smyth—

specious excuse or another, to leading men of the day. Mr Gladstone was favoured with a horrible sonnet on the Bulgarian atrocities, and a flattering letter which blamed its composition on to the Grand Old Man's moving oratory. Gladstone was incautious enough to reply sympathetically, and was immediately shot into silence with an even worse sonnet.

Several men of letters received the sonnet and essay on Keats' grave which Wilde had published in Dublin. The penultimate line of the sonnet offers a rare example of the occasional lapse into an Irish accent which his friends observed in Oscar at the time: the rhythm suggests that he may have pronounced 'our' as two separate syllables:

> But our tears shall keep thy memory green,
> And make it flourish like a Basil-tree.

The most important of Wilde's epistolary self-introductions at this time was to Walter Pater, the shy prophet of beauty, whose fame as a writer of ornately precious prose was curiously undonnish in a fellow of Brasenose. Wilde wrote to him, visited him, admired him, learned from him, imitated his prose style on occasions, and always valued his good opinion highly. He accepted from Pater the important Aesthetic doctrine that life should be filled with perfectly beautiful experiences, since the beautiful is in itself good. Later he was to confuse this (in a quite common manner) with the contradictory doctrine that beauty is entirely separate from ethical value, and must be cultivated in works of art with a firm disregard for moral questions.

John Ruskin was Wilde's other great Oxford mentor. He was at this time Slade Professor of Fine Art, and Wilde learned from him all he could about technical art criticism. He observed, too, that Ruskin, like Pater, gave added weight to his opinions by taking care that they were always expressed in striking prose. Although Wilde was subsequently to claim that he had participated in the Hinksey road-building venture through which Ruskin hoped to teach the young men of Oxford a sense of social duty, it seems unlikely that this was the case. The road was started before Wilde went up to Oxford, and there is nothing to suggest that he would have pushed himself forward as a first-year undergraduate. When later reminding Ruskin of their master and pupil relationship at Oxford Wilde referred to nothing more than 'walks and talks'. And according to Frank Harris, Ruskin remembered Wilde as one of those who scoffed at the road-building.

The dominating teacher in Wilde's life, in fact, was still Mahaffy. At the end of his first year in Oxford, Wilde visited Italy with his old Trinity tutor. It was an uneventful journey, from which he wrote home the usual young raptures over Italian art, and a few severe archaeological observations for his father's benefit. In the spring of his third year a more important journey with Mahaffy took place. Wilde was to pass the early part of the Easter vacation in Greece with Mahaffy, and then travel alone to Rome, where his Magdalen friends hoped he might have an audience with the Pope and become a Catholic once and for all. Wilde himself looked forward to the dangerous titillation of religion in Rome like a maiden hoping she *may* be seduced by a notorious old rake. Mahaffy was, no doubt, sharp enough to see what his old pupil's writhing determination to see Rome augured, and with firm pagan sense dragged him off on an extended tour of Athens and Mycenae, so that there was little time left for the seductions of St Peter's. When Rome was finally visited, it all seemed a little anticlimactic after the glories of Greece under Mahaffy's inspired guidance. Oscar came back rather shamefacedly to Magdalen with his Protestant maidenhead intact.

He also came back to trouble with the college authorities. Mahaffy's extension of the tour had caused Wilde to miss a week of the summer term, and he was sent down for what was left of it. Quite rightly, Wilde was outraged at this pettifogging punishment, which suggested that college residence statutes had more to do with education than a chance of visiting Greece with one of the leading scholars of the day. Mahaffy, too, resented the implied slight offered by men with far less ability than he. Wilde had seen something of the pettiness and jealousy that can lie beneath Oxford's smoothly civilized veneer, and he took no further interest in the possibility of a fellowship.

From then on he used Oxford adroitly, and wrung all the honour and notoriety he could from it. He continued to love it as a place, and thoroughly enjoyed the time he passed there. But he dismissed the idea of a career in which his own large-minded generosity might be brought into conflict with the quarrelsome meannesses of an unchanging set of colleagues.

His standing in Magdalen was thoroughly restored by the end of his final year, when he won the Newdigate Prize for poetry. The subject set by the examiners was *Ravenna*, which he had happily visited with Mahaffy. Wilde revelled in the requirement that he give a public recitation of his rather stiff poem in the presence of the Vice-Chancellor and university dignitaries in the Sheldonian Theatre.

A month later his First in Greats was confirmed, and Magdalen extended his demyship for a fifth year. But apart from a half-hearted attempt to win another university prize, he made little use of this. Before 1879 was out he had left Oxford.

Oscar Wilde–the aesthetic student poet of
his last years at Oxford.

'PROFESSOR of AESTHETICS'

'A new Hedonism – that is what our century wants. You might be its visible symbol. With your personality there is nothing you could not do. The world belongs to you for a season.'

The next three years laid the firm foundations of the legendary Oscar Wilde. Whether he really did and said all the things attributed to him at this time cannot be established with certainty. Whether he really wore outrageous clothes as a mark of Aestheticism is not clear. He himself said that he had *not* walked through the streets of London carrying a lily, but had made the world *believe* that he did – a far more difficult matter.

Certainly it was a time in which he was striving for the maximum self-advertisement, while not actually doing very much. He badly wanted to be a public figure, and did not mind if notoriety preceded fame. But he had no particular career in mind, although after 1880 he was to make several abortive attempts to follow the example of an older dandiacal poet, Matthew Arnold, and become a schools inspector.

He was helped by the Philistinism of the middle class public, which only wanted a representative figure against whom to direct its hatred of artistic pretensions. If Oscar Wilde wanted to appear before London as an exemplary outrageous art-lover, *Punch* had already drawn a simple blue-print for him. George du Maurier had begun an amusing series of cartoons on the affectations of high culture, based on the utterances of the salon hostess 'Mrs Cimabue Brown', and her two lions, 'Maudle the painter and Jellaby Postlethwaite the poet'. *Punch* also drew un-named 'poet' figures to a standard pattern. The real target was a never-actually-named Swinburne. The *Punch* model had long hair, thin legs in breeches, flowing upper garments, and a mysterious habit of swooning over flowers.

Wilde took the hint, and made sure that his public image fitted Philistia's preconceived image of 'the poet'. He let his hair grow much longer than it had been in Oxford – a sure way of attracting unintelligent attention and abuse. He had made a striking impression at a fancy dress ball in Oxford when he arrived as Prince Rupert of the Rhine. Now he turned this success to public advantage, claiming that cavalier costume was the perfect clothing for men, and wearing breeches and velvet jackets to evening parties. He adopted Byron's mode of soft, turned-down shirt collars, and became rather particular about his colourful, loose neckties. And he asserted that all this was sorely-needed dress reform. Philistia knew better, and could recognise a poseur when it saw one. 'There goes that bloody fool, Oscar Wilde,' grumbled a testy gentleman who saw him in the street. Oscar was delighted: 'It's extraordinary how soon one gets known in London,' he remarked to his companion.

He became increasingly widely known. Jellaby Postlethwaite and Maudle had been comically gauche and untidy in du Maurier's original conception. But gradually they came to be given the large build and distinctive features of Oscar Wilde. When Gilbert and Sullivan gave the world *Patience*, it was taken for granted that the main target was Wilde, although Gilbert had actually looked first to Swinburne for inspiration when he came to turn his satire against poets.

Wilde also sought to be known as the friend and admirer of the loveliest women of the day. Among society ladies, he valued the friendship and patronage of Lord Ronald Gower's sister, the Duchess of Westminster, and young Lady Lonsdale. But when he spoke of being with 'beautiful people' – a favourite phrase of his at this time – it was likely to be Lillie Langtry, Ellen Terry, Sarah Bernhardt, or even Helena Modjeska that he had in mind.

'The Jersey Lily' took her famous nickname from Millais's portrait of her with that title. Born Emily Charlotte le Breton, she was brought from Jersey clerical society into the Prince of Wales's circle by her husband, Edward Langtry. Her generation thought her the most beautiful woman in London, and she sat for painters like Whistler, Watts, Burne-Jones and Leighton.

THE SIX-MARK TEA-POT.

Æsthetic Bridegroom. "It is quite consummate, is it not?"
Intense Bride. "It is, indeed! Oh, Algernon, let us live up to it!"

NINCOMPOOPIANA.—THE MUTUAL ADMIRATION SOCIETY.

Our Gallant Colonel (who is not a Member thereof, to Mrs. Cimabue Brown, who is). "And who's this young Hero they're all swarming over now?"
Mrs. Cimabue Brown. "Jellaby Postlethwaite, the great Poet, you know, who sat for Maudle's 'Dead Narcissus'! He has just dedicated his Latter-Day Sapphics to me. Is not he Beautiful?"
Our Gallant Colonel. "Why, what's there Beautiful about him?"
Mrs. Cimabue Brown. "Oh, look at his Grand Head and Poetic Face, with those Flowerlike Eyes, and that Exquisite Sad Smile! Look at his Slender Willowy Frame, as yielding and fragile as a Woman's! That's young Maudle, standing just behind him—the great Painter, you know. He has just painted Me as 'Héloïse,' and my Husband as 'Abélard.' Is not he Divine!"
N.B.—*Postlethwaite and Maudle are quite unknown to fame.* [*The Colonel hooks it.*]

left Oscar Wilde claimed to have said this of his blue china at Oxford…

…and many people believed he had voiced Postlethwaite's view of bathing.

above and below Du Maurier's spoof artist and poet began as anonymous grotesques…

…but soon came to wear Wilde's features and adopt his attitudes.

POSTLETHWAITE ON "REFRACTION."

Grigsby. "Hullo, my Jellaby, you here! Come and take a dip in the Briny, old Man. I'm sure you look as if you wanted it!"
Postlethwaite. "Thanks, no. I never bathe. I always see myself so dreadfully foreshortened in the Water, you know!"

MAUDLE ON THE CHOICE OF A PROFESSION.

Maudle. "How consummately lovely your Son is, Mrs. Brown!"
Mrs. Brown (a Philistine from the country). "What? He's a nice, manly Boy, if you mean that, Mr. Maudle. He has just left School, you know, and wishes to be an Artist."
Maudle. "Why should he be an Artist?"
Mrs. Brown. "Well, he must be something!"
Maudle. "Why should he be anything? Why not let him remain for ever content to Exist Beautifully?"
[*Mrs. Brown determines that at all events her Son shall not study Art under Maudle.*

right The Jersey Lily. Three heads of Lillie Langtry by Frank Miles, with an aesthetic background of lilies.

below Frank Miles, the artist friend of Wilde's who shared living space with him in rooms in Salisbury Street off the Strand. He died in an insane asylum in 1891.

below right Lady Lonsdale, one of Oscar's society friends. When she was widowed in the early 1890s, Speranza entertained a fleeting hope that she might marry Oscar.

Oscar Wilde had taken rooms off the Strand, in Salisbury Street, with his friend Frank Miles, and Mrs Langtry was one of Miles's favourite subjects. It was a suitably attention-drawing gesture for Wilde to publish bad sonnets to Lillie, clumsily calling her 'Helen, formerly of Troy, now of London'. And Mrs Langtry's public identification with the floral emblem of purity which recurred obsessively in Pre-Raphaelite painting fitted well with her poet's publicly maintained belief that the lily and the sunflower were the perfect models of natural beauty.

At the same time it should be remembered that Lillie Langtry, like Lady Lonsdale, was a young woman moving in the powerful circles of her older husband's contemporaries. Furthermore Lillie, like Oscar, came from a middle-class background in the provinces (if Dublin may be so described), and was now having to hold her own in aristocratic metropolitan society. These two young people might well find each other's company and friendship a relaxation in the strenuous life of social climbing, and having different goals, aptitudes and genders they were not rivals.

The other three women with whom Oscar was careful to link his name were actresses of international distinction. Helena Modjeska, the oldest of the three, was a Polish actress with a powerful romantic style. She made her London

debut in 1880 to an audience which included the Prince of Wales. We may be fairly sure that it also included Oscar Wilde, an assiduous first-nighter and fringe-frequenter of the Prince of Wales's circle.

Soon Madame Modjeska was having to tell Wilde that it would be indiscreet for her to visit his rooms, even for tea. But not long after that she allowed him to publish his own translation of one of her Polish poems, thereby posing a minor mystery: where and when did Oscar learn any Polish? The answer is that probably he did not. Publishing translations from an astonishing range of languages had been a habit of Speranza's for years, though her own command of the original tongues was in some doubt. Oscar probably found out from Madame Modjeska what her poem was about, and may even have glanced at a few words in a dictionary, before making himself 'the reed through which her sweet notes have been blown'.

Ellen Terry was perhaps the sweetest of Oscar's bevy of beauty. He was fortunate in the time at which he launched himself at London. Ellen's great partnership with Henry Irving at the Lyceum, which was to dominate London theatre for the next twenty years, had only just begun. Ten years later she might well have been beyond the young poet's reach, and Irving would certainly have been a lion too grand for Oscar to solicit his autograph on behalf

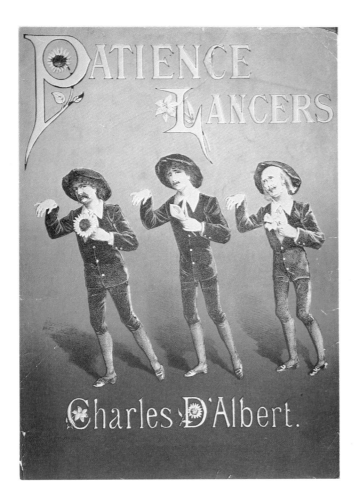

above Gilbert and Sullivan's *Patience* was produced in the spring of 1881 and everyone enjoyed the joke about aesthetic poets and poetry. Oscar Wilde enjoyed it too, and turned it to very good account, as did the composers of popular sheet music.

above right *The Annunciation* by Dante Gabriel Rossetti. The Pre-Raphaelites seemed to have an obsession with lilies, and this neatly fitted Oscar's purpose. He always declared, however, that he had not – like Bunthorne – carried a lily; but he made people believe that he had, a much more difficult thing. Tate Gallery.

far right Blue and white china, which Oscar declared he felt a need to 'live up to', owed its vogue to the French artists and connoisseurs of the 1850s, who discovered the elegance and beauty of oriental art. Whistler fostered the vogue in England, and featured oriental china in this painting of 1864. John G. Johnson Collection, Philadelphia.

of William Morris's daughter. But the king and
queen of the acting world had only moved into their
palace in 1878. Ellen's good nature made her easily
accessible to an importunate and charming young
man, and Irving's love for her meant that the great
man would invite the young poet to his splendid
opening-night banquets. Oscar even wrote a sonnet
for him.

Ellen Terry was a suitable friend for a writer who
was trying to base a part of his reputation on his
knowledge of modern art. Her life had been
constantly connected with the art world, and painters
loved her as a subject almost as much as they loved
Mrs Langtry. After an early mismarriage to the
painter G. F. Watts, Ellen had lived for six years
with E. W. Godwin, the architect who designed
Whistler's house in Chelsea, and was later to advise
Wilde on the decoration of his second Tite Street
home.

Ellen's first house in London had been decorated
by Godwin in the ultra-modern Aesthetic style that
succeeded Pre-Raphaelitism when the influence of
the cool colours and simple design of Japanese art
began to be felt. Her drawing-room floor was
covered with straw-coloured matting and supported
plain wicker-work furniture. The walls were white,
hung with grey-blue cretonne. A life-sized cast of the
Venus de Milo stood in the centre of the room.
It is too easily forgotten that the Forsytean hugger-
mugger of fussily upholstered mahogany that
cluttered so many late Victorian houses was
challenged, in artistic circles, by interior decoration
of great simplicity and charm. Oscar and 'Nelly'
(as Ellen soon became to him) would have agreed on
the nature of a pleasant room.

Another link with Nelly was Florence Balcombe.
The Bram Stokers had joined Irving's entourage
after the young Irishman had impressed the actor-
manager by bursting into hysterics on hearing him
recite Hood's melodramatic poem *Eugene Aram*.
Anyone with such discrimination and taste would
obviously have practical financial acumen, and it was
as Irving's business manager that Stoker was best
known to London. Florence meekly accepted
occasional walking-on parts in Lyceum productions,
and Oscar, doubtless dramatising suitably, told Ellen
of his former passion for the young Irishwoman.
He preserved the romantic interest of the situation
by using Ellen to transmit flowers anonymously to
Florence when she was appearing. And of course he
cemented his relations with Ellen herself by sending
flowers to her, and celebrating her publicly in bad
sonnets.

Sarah Bernhardt was the perfect object of Oscar's
adoration. She was quite as flamboyant as he, and
quite as close to the world of art as Ellen Terry.

below A photograph of Lillie Langtry. Her
friendship with the Prince of Wales took
Oscar into the fringes of royal society.

bottom Helene Modjeska, the distinguished
Polish actress, another one of the ladies of
international fame who became a friend of
Wilde's. He translated one of her poems into
English. Modjeska is seen here as Portia.

Sarah Bernhardt in 1879, in a portrait
by Jules Bastien-Lepage. This is how the
great actress looked when Oscar Wilde first
met her.

left Ellen Terry as Lady Macbeth, from the painting by John Singer Sargent. 'Ellen, how *could* you?' called Oscar from his front door in Tite Street, seeing her drive past in costume for a sitting. 'Oscar, how *dare* you!' she replied.

far left Sarah Bernhardt, seen by *Vanity Fair*. Unlike Ellen Terry, her great contemporary, Sarah enjoyed a romantic delight in continuing her performances off stage.

As Pre-Raphaelitism was transposed through Aestheticism into Art Nouveau, Sarah Bernhardt emerged as the living muse of the movement. She was painted and sculpted, and she painted and sculpted herself. She kept her own studio, and wore comfortably elegant trouser suits sixty years before any other fashionable woman dared to. She was, genuinely, a great romantic actress: it was by sheer talent that she took Paris by storm. But she had the romantic Thespian's delight in continuing the performance off-stage; undoubtedly she gave delight to many people thereby and harmed none. Like Oscar she enjoyed to the full turning her life-style and public image into a form of art. It is thus very difficult to know, between the exaggerations and embroideries of the two of them, exactly what their relationship was in those early days.

Sarah claimed that she heard two voices above the crowds at Folkestone, when she landed in England with the Comédie Française company for the first time. Johnston Forbes-Robertson's unusually beautiful tones thrilled her with words she claimed she had never heard before–'Vive Sarah Bernhardt!' Oscar Wilde, 'the leading young poet in England', was also unusually imaginative: 'Hip hip hurrah! A cheer for Sarah Bernhardt!' he is supposed to have said. Next, as Sarah recalled it, he threw a carpet of lilies at her feet. She said nothing about Mrs Langtry's unkind suggestion that Oscar adopted the amaryllis lily as his emblem because it was beautiful in single blooms, and so he was spared the expense of presenting whole bouquets to visiting beauties. It would have been inartistic to suggest it: she had just acknowledged a single gardenia from Forbes-Robertson.

While she stayed in England, Oscar willingly fussed around her, helped her win publicity, and may well have undertaken small secretarial duties for her as he occasionally did for Mrs. Langtry. Naturally he wrote her a bad sonnet. And he entertained her at parties in Salisbury Street. At these high spirits were always likely to triumph over aesthetic languor, as on the splendid occasion when Sarah took a stick of Frank Miles's charcoal, and sportingly tried to write her name as high up the wall as she could reach by jumping.

Since Oscar's notorious public style at this time was flagrantly 'high camp', and some doubtful whispers about his sexual propensities had circulated at Oxford, it might seem strange that he should have a contradictory reputation for attracting female adoration. Actually there was no real contradiction. Oscar's mode of drawing attention to himself involved fastidiousness, languor, flamboyance, hypersensitivity, and a supercilious disregard for the cruder denominators of virility. But he did not

Punch's rejection of Oscar Wilde's poems.

" O. W."

" O, I feel just as happy as a bright Sunflower !'
Lays of Christy Minstrelsy.

Æsthete of Æsthetes !
What 's in a name ?
The poet is WILDE,
But his poetry 's tame.

assume feminine characteristics, giggle, or use feminine pronouns about himself and any homosexual friends. In fact there was nothing particularly homosexual about the form of wit and public attitudinising we now call 'high camp' until its leading practitioner had been publicly convicted of sodomy. The drawling camp style had been common in the eighteenth century, and was revived from time to time in the nineteenth by various dandies protesting against uncouth masculinity. Perhaps its finest exponent before Oscar Wilde was the young Disraeli, who of course was exclusively heterosexual. Oscar Wilde, as we know, was an admirer of Disraeli's writings, which contain heroic models of camp behaviour. Ladies in the 1870s were free to enjoy the wit of an exponent of camp, and to recognise in his insouciant arrogance and peacock display the masculine assertiveness required to give a sexual edge to their admiration. Oscar Wilde, like his parody, Bunthorne in *Patience,* was genuinely attractive to women, and partly for the very good reason that like Disraeli he was unusual in the male chauvinist society of his day in that he truly enjoyed women's company and respected women as people.

But did Wilde really desire women as sexual objects? He had shown himself aware of homosexuality at Oxford, using the euphemism 'psychological' to signal to friends in the know that he was talking about gay matters. The rumour that he was a 'Miss Nancy' had reached America by 1880, and most sophisticated Parisians thought when they first saw Wilde that he was not entirely heterosexual. For what it is worth there is also the evidence that some ladies found him repulsive: Lady Colin Campbell, for example, called him 'The Great White Slug'. This has led to a recent suggestion that Wilde was consistently and exclusively homosexual; that the affair with Florence Balcombe was mere affectation without attraction; and that Frank Miles was Wilde's sexual partner as well as room-mate.

An immediate objection to this thesis lies in the fact that the whisper about Miles was not that he liked men, but that he liked very young girls – notably fifteen-year-old Sally Higgs who acted as parlour-maid at the Salisbury Street bachelor establishment. It is impossible to substantiate at this date, of course, and Miles was a mysterious figure, who once ran away from the police out of the back of the apartment while Oscar held the front door closed. Later the two quarrelled irrevocably, and in 1891 Miles died in an asylum.

The notion that Oscar Wilde was in any way homosexual before 1886 was at one time scouted by his friends and acquaintances. They roundly asserted that he first experimented with boys when he was thirty-two, and became exclusively homosexual three years later. But this theory, too, seems rather too cut-and-dried, and has certainly been adopted rather thoughtlessly by writers who wished to express animus against Robbie Ross, the young homosexual who became Wilde's closest friend and disciple in 1886.

It seems more reasonable to suppose that Wilde's sexual identity was in a state of immature confusion until his early thirties: that up to this time he was potentially – and probably actually – bisexual. His passion for Florence was real, and genuinely grounded on some sexual attraction even if, like all his emotions at this time, it was slightly superficial, and substantially dramatised for effect. There is no doubt at all that he understood and shared the public admiration for Lillie Langtry's beauty, and he once told a friend that his love for Lillie had prevented him from falling in love with Sarah Bernhardt, which he would otherwise have done. At the same time he certainly had known a little more than might be expected about the homosexual fraternity at Oxford, and appeared to feel that he and one of his Magdalen friends had something to conceal from others. And if it is true that Lord Ronald Gower and Frank Miles were well-known members of gay circles in London when Wilde met them, then the case for a bisexual young Oscar is very strong indeed.

Meanwhile Willie was doing his best to further his brilliant young brother's career. The sale of Merrion Square brought Willie and his mother over to Mayfair where in Park Street, as a few years later in Oakley Street, Chelsea, Lady Wilde's receptions tried vainly to recapture the position Speranza's salon had held in Dublin society. Wilde had the family capacity to wield a pen, and with some introductions from Dublin he began to work as a hack journalist. *The World,* edited by Dickens's former protégé Edmund Yates, was a platform for much fashionable and artistic gossip: Whistler and Oscar Wilde were to cross swords in its pages. And Willie contributed gossipy notes to it which featured as often as possible the doings of Oscar, the self-styled 'Professor of Aesthetics'. At Park Street, Speranza made her sons the lions of her crowded, dimly-lit receptions. New arrivals from Dublin could always be relied upon to pay her a visit, and hear about her brilliant boys. And even for Londoners these quaint occasions held some curiosity-value at first.

For all three Wildes, money was tight. Speranza, with a heroic disregard for her revolutionary past, applied to Disraeli's Conservative government for a pension. Naturally it was refused, but there was some satisfaction for the generally forgotten and eccentric old lady in the fact that she could still be martyred for the old cause. Willie was hopelessly careless with money, and depended on his mother to keep his

right Walt Whitman. Oscar visited the great
American poet in Camden, New Jersey, and
the occasion gave pleasure to both. Whitman
liked his visitor, gave him home-made wine,
and praised him to the press.

*below Nocturne, Blue and Silver. Cremorne
Lights.* Whistler's enthusiasm for Japanese
art is plainly reflected in this famous painting.
Tate Gallery.

Richard D'Oyly Carte, from a
lithograph by Spy in *Vanity Fair*, 1891. The
impresario of the Gilbert and Sullivan operas,
he organised Wilde's American tour as
publicity for *Patience* in 1882.

affairs in any sort of order. Oscar had to sell his houses at Bray, move out of the elegant white-and-yellow apartment in Salisbury Street to the cheaper No. 1, Tite Street, and finally scrape together his poems for publication. He had to pay the publisher's expenses, but his self-advertisement had been so successful that despite a poor critical reception the volume ran through four editions, making him a pleasant little profit, and relieving him of the necessity of referring back to the Newdigate Prize to justify his poetic standing.

Oscar Wilde was a successful but very minor poet. His verse evinced a pompous wish to pontificate, yet a total lack of any clear stance from which to do so. Libertarian poems asserting republican ideals recurred, yet a major effort was the long *Ave Imperatrix*, celebrating the might of the British Empire. Was Wilde an Irish nationalist or a loyal West Briton? Probably he could not have given a consistent answer to this question for two weeks running. He was not really a political animal, although like his mother he thoroughly enjoyed the enthusiastic fervour associated with a 'cause', and might momentarily persuade himself that he accepted its principles. It was characteristic of his inconsistency (as well as his naive careerism) that he should hopefully send a complimentary copy of his poems to Gladstone with a letter flattering his statesmanship, although he had for some time been making very full use of the Conservative and Constitutional St Stephen's Club, which he had joined from Oxford.

The political poems, however, did strike reviewers as suitably earnest. More dubious were his romantic effusions. Like most young poets Wilde was so strongly influenced by the work he admired that his own work often sounded like a poor parody. He was capable of echoing very famous lines with an apparent temporary oblivion of the originals. And passages that he hoped were sheer beauty were the merest imitation of Keats and Tennyson.

The greatest danger to his reputation came from the long ambitious *Charmides*, which retold in lush Keatsian diction the classical myth of the youth who fell in love with a statue of Athena, and was struck dead by the goddess for uncovering the statue's nakedness. Wilde brought out the erotic potential of the story as strongly as possible, introducing a note of unusually overt sexuality into Victorian poetry. Of course he went to no extreme that could have shocked or even surprised any reader familiar with nineteenth-century French poetry. But such dangerous decadence was unfamiliar to English readers and the godly were not lacking to spring up and accuse Wilde of immoral writing. The intellectual but not-so-godly young men of the

James McNeill Whistler, painter, wit, dandy, was mentor and friend to Oscar Wilde – at first. But Whistler would not brook any challenge to his self-assumed right to primacy in the field of artistic opinion, and the friendship later turned to enmity. From a drawing by Rajoir.

right Gilbert and Sullivan's opera *Patience* ridiculed the 'fleshly', or sensuous poetry of Swinburne and Wilde, and the feminine admiration it won. Wilde accepted the notoriety the satire brought him, and continued to recommend knee-breeches for men, Grecian costume for women, and the Grosvenor Gallery's exhibitions of new and aesthetic art.

ye indifference of ye Dragoons.

ye aestheti-cally poet

ye dairy maid

ye GREENERY-YALLERY GROSVENOR GALLERY ONE

ye FAITHFUL ONE

YE LEGEND OF YE MAGNET & YE CHURN.

above Oscar Wilde in 1884. A caricature by Ape in *Vanity Fair*.

left Whistler's famous Peacock Room. Oscar praised the design in extravagant terms during his lecture tour in America. Charles Freer bought the panelled room from a London dealer in 1904 and it is now in the Freer Gallery of Art, Washington, D.C.

Oxford Union refused their presentation copy on the grounds that there was more plagiarism than original creation in the volume. *Punch* triumphantly crowed:

The poet is Wilde
But the poetry's tame.

The volume was sent to influential places to further the *arriviste* campaign. Robert Browning and Matthew Arnold each received a copy with a flattering little note from the author. Wilde tried to make sure that some reviews at least were by friends who would be certain to show a favourable bias. The greatest living poet, Gerard Manley Hopkins, bought his copy privately, and recorded his disappointment in it privately. But he was a very private figure: an Oxford Jesuit, whose work would not be known till after his death. Wilde was unaware that this far greater poetic pupil of Pater's lived, creating great poetry on Catholic and Paterian lines.

The move to Tite Street brought Wilde and Miles within the immediate orbit of James McNeill Whistler, the fiery leader of *avant-garde* painting. Whistler was an American, though he repeatedly denied the fact that he had been born in Lowell, Massachussetts, and sometimes posed as a southern gentleman. He had hoped to fight in the American Civil War, but had gone instead to Paris to train as a painter, carrying with him a considerable stock of unsubdued belligerency. He delighted in the cruel epigram and the mocking gibe. His victims were expected to conceal their embarrassment and join him in a sharply barked laugh, though he cared not at all if they were really wounded. He had early discovered a way of drawing an elegant butterfly with pointed wings and a curving tail, in which the initials JMW could be dimly discerned, and used this rebus as his monogram. As he grew older and more sardonically bitter the butterfly's tail developed an increasingly pronounced and appropriate scorpion's sting.

Whistler was happy to accept the notorious young poet as a disciple and he had much to teach him. First and foremost he was to discipline Oscar's visual taste, or at least lead it into perfected avenues of fashion. It was pre-eminently Whistler who had 'discovered' Japanese art for London, allowed it to influence his own work, and started the craze for collecting blue and white china. Colours were important to him. He outraged the middle class public by giving paintings that were obviously portraits such titles as *Study in Black and Yellow*. His own favourite colour, egg-yolk yellow, became the most fashionable shade for interior decoration, and ultimately came to seem the tint which best summed up the art of a decade when *The Yellow Book* adopted it.

If Wilde was never more than a moderately apt pupil in matters of taste – his private preference for the flamboyant was always in danger of overriding Whistler's sense of harmony and restraint – he was the perfect disciple for Whistler's theory of art. Whistler was a monumental egotist. *He* was an artist. He was *the* artist. Art was (therefore) more important than anything else in the world. The views of fools and blunderers who had not dedicated their lives to art (were not *the* artist) should be utterly disregarded. Indeed, it was positively meritorious to offend them. For art and *the* artist rose above society, nature and morality. What fools thought unappealing, unrealistic, or distasteful in a true work of art (or painting by Whistler) merely served to show their own incapacity to appreciate true beauty, and thus their total unfitness to venture any opinion at all on anything.

Now Oscar Wilde, although highly egotistical himself, was far too generous a person to understand the rancorous self-aggrandisement and defensiveness that lay behind Whistler's pronouncements. Wilde really liked other people, and valued their esteem and goodwill, so that whatever he might say about the artist owing no duty to the public, in practice he never made the mistake of imagining that artistic creations offered in the open market existed independently of any audience. Whistler, who feared and disliked everybody else in the world, had devised a theory that cushioned his own ego by proving that nobody else mattered. Wilde, recognising Whistler's essential seriousness or earnestness, and perhaps knowing that a profound commitment to art rather than a superficial commitment to celebrity was above all what he lacked himself, adopted Whistler's supreme evaluation of art and the artist. It seemed but a small step forward from the *l'art pour l'art* position which Pater had developed. But Wilde lacked the philosophical prestidigitation by which Pater confused beauty with virtue. And so he had shifted his thinking from the undeniable position that technical judgement is the only judgement permitted in technical matters, to the indefensible position that technical values are themselves the highest of all possible values. Thus he became a leading spokesman for the doctrine of 'Art for art's sake', and said many interesting things in its defence, while at first overlooking the untenability of his basic philosophy.

The greatest lesson Whistler had to teach his pupil was an improvement in personal style. Wilde had mastered effrontery on his own. Whistler was to sharpen his wits, teach him to use epigram offensively, and show him the tone of perfect heartlessness essential to perfect dandyism. Of course Wilde did not go the whole way with Whistler; he did not actually regard the world with contempt. But he learned to behave as if he did; he learned the value of the quick riposte; he learned the art of polishing a *mot* to perfection, and steering a conversation to the point where it could be produced with apparent spontaneity. And he learned not to waste his best phrases but to use them again and again. He followed Whistler's example in sending copies of his most amusing telegrams to *The World*. So the public shared their exchanges when *Punch* parodied their conversation:

Wilde to Whistler: *Punch* too ridiculous. When you and I are together we never talk about anything but ourselves.

Whistler to Wilde: No, no, Oscar, you forget. When you and I are together we never talk about anything except me.

Wilde to Whistler: It is true, Jimmy, we were talking about you, but I was thinking of myself.

In the early days of their acquaintance Wilde was happy to learn from the older man, and never thought seriously of challenging the little Mephisophelean dandy's right to primacy in the field of artistic opinion. For, notwithstanding Oscar Wilde was well enough known to figure in the foreground of Frith's painting of *Varnishing Day at the Royal Academy* (outranking even such notables as Henry Irving and Ellen Terry), he was still only a small celebrity who had achieved almost nothing since he left Oxford. America was to provide him with his first taste of deserved success.

Varnishing Day at the Royal Academy by W. P. Frith, 1881. Oscar can be seen right of centre, with an open catalogue in his hand.

AMERICA

'The youth of America is their oldest tradition. It has been going on now for three hundred years. To hear them talk one would imagine they were in their first childhood. As far as civilization goes they are in their second.'

Gilbert and Sullivan's *Patience* was produced in the spring of 1881. Oscar Wilde went to the first night, and being very good-natured, thoroughly enjoyed the joke against himself. In the autumn, D'Oyly Carte, the producer, arranged for its presentation in New York. There was one problem: Aesthetes and Aesthetic poetry were unknown in the U.S.A. Would Americans get the joke?

Colonel Morse, D'Oyly Carte's American agent, suggested that it might help the opera's box office if Oscar the Aesthete himself could be persuaded to cross the Atlantic and give a series of lectures in towns where *Patience* was to be performed. Morse was an experienced lecture tour organiser and there seemed a reasonable chance that a useful profit might be made by all concerned. Oscar, having no other immediate prospects, agreed.

He had accepted a very difficult challenge. His tour was an obvious promotional stunt. It accorded ill with the dignity he claimed for poetry, art, and his own opinions. He had no experience whatsoever of lecturing, and was going to a country where the lecture was one of the most familiar and popular forms of entertainment. The American press was less restrained than the English, and even that had become accustomed to treating Oscar as good comic copy. And he was going to lecture on art, from the standpoint of a cosmopolitan urban man. His audience came from a country which looked rather like a vast expanse of unusually Philistine provinces tacked on to a thin eastern strip of imitative culture. Under these depressing circumstances it is immensely to his credit that he emerged from his American tour with his reputation enhanced. He might have been expected to return home sheepishly after a fiasco (whose publicity would have suited D'Oyly Carte as well as a success). Instead he won the plaudits of every one who mattered.

First there were preparations to be made. Hermann Vezin, the actor, gave his young friend a few lessons in voice production. A theatrical costumier supplied a pair of knee-breeches, and stockings with splendid clocks. It was only fair to D'Oyly Carte to give him a bit of Bunthorne for his backing. A vast fur-lined, fur-collared overcoat was also to be bought as protection against the American winter. It became one of Oscar's best-loved possessions, though Whistler pretended to believe that it, too, was a theatrical property, and urged him to return it to Nathan's.

On Christmas Eve 1881 Oscar Wilde boarded the *Arizona*. As became an Aesthetic poet he held himself a little aloof, and looked melancholy and dispirited. He did not (his fellow-passengers observed) use the popular catch-phrases which were supposed to be the mark of the Aesthete – 'too too' and 'utter', both used in a somewhat absolute rather than intensive sense. Wilde spoke English, not comic Gilbertese. Nor on this occasion did he employ the fashionable jargon words which were a part of his vocabulary – 'precious' and 'intense' – because both were praise words, and he found little to praise in the Atlantic.

When the boat docked at New York, his fellow-passengers told the press that Oscar Wilde had said the Atlantic was disappointing, and this being more newsworthy than anything the poet had said in person was flashed around the world as if it were an eccentric opinion. At the customs stage Oscar picked up more energy, and did a little better with his famous confession, 'I have nothing to declare. Except my genius.' 'That, sir,' replied the customs officer, 'is a commodity which does not require protection in the United States.'

A week later Oscar gave his first lecture on *The English Renaissance*. His audience at Chickering Hall, New York, was delighted to see that he wore long hair and knee-breeches but a little disappointed that he carried no sunflower. The lecturer's manner was poor. His well-modulated tenor voice, which in later

Part of a page from *Punch*, 4 February 1882, saying farewell to Oscar Wilde. The text drew attention to Wilde's already apparent gourmandizing.

them he would become deserving of American attention as a serious commentator on the arts.

The English Renaissance, which was to be heard by audiences right across the country, was Wilde's first sustained piece of critical thought. His subject was nineteenth-century English art. Keats, who had written 'Beauty is truth, truth beauty,—that is all Ye know on earth, and all ye need to know', was the parent and inspiration of the great revival of art in England. The Pre-Raphaelite painters and poets—Rossetti, Burne-Jones, Morris—were its centre, and Tennyson and Swinburne were its poetic flowering. All these artists shared a common dedication to beauty for its own sake. They rejected (according to Wilde) the view that poetry or art could or should devote itself to the examination of social or moral problems. Their work was the creation of objects which pleased by virtue of their tranquil harmony. And therefore they were truer artists than Byron and Wordsworth, who made the mistake of using poetry as a platform or a pulpit. Beauty alone was timeless and unchanging. It was separate and remote from the world of action, yet it was only by stepping aside and enjoying the refreshment offered by self-possessed works of harmonious beauty that active civilisations could achieve nobility. 'We spend our days,' the lecturer concluded, 'each one of us, in looking for the secret of life. Well, the secret of life is in art.'

The press took no notice of the content of Wilde's lecture, but continued to treat him as a buffoon. Nevertheless, serious listeners were impressed, and failed to object to one obvious weakness the lecturer was slipping into: a habit of using 'British' as a term of abuse. 'To disagree with three-fourths of the British public on all points is one of the first elements of sanity,' was a typical utterance. In the context of a lecture delivered in New York it might seem a crude appeal to American anglophobia; but it represented a mental habit of unconsidered anti-patriotism which was to give Kipling and Henley fuel for their fierce dislike of Wilde and his circle.

Outside the columns of the press and the fatigues of the lecture hall, Oscar was having a great social success. He aroused hysterical feminine enthusiasm which reached a climax at an absurd dinner party where he was the only man present. To the eighteen fashionable girls hanging on his every word he expatiated on the beauty of the roses which decorated the table. At the end of the meal he made a silly pun: 'America reminds me of one of Edgar Allan Poe's exquisite poems,' he remarked, 'because it is full of belles.' Seizing this cue, one of the girls tossed a rose at him, crying, 'Behold, the tribute of the belles!' The others took it up, and Oscar sat fatuously in the shower of roses flung from around the table.

life would become rich and plummy, lacked the full resonance to which American audiences were accustomed. He read his words directly from the rather beautiful hand-bound script in front of him. He was not very funny, and in spite of his careful flattery of American sensibilities the audience was bored.

And yet, for Oscar Wilde this was a success. His lecture had been essentially serious, and intelligent people realised that he deserved to be taken seriously. His hair and breeches were his only bow to vulgar publicity. If he could attract an audience without

DISTINGUISHED AMATEURS.—2. THE ART-CRITIC.

Prigsby (contemplating his friend Maudle's last Picture). "THE HEAD OF ALEXIS IS DISTINCTLY DIVINE! NOR CAN *I*, IN THE WHOLE RANGE OF ANCIENT, MEDIÆVAL, OR MODERN ART, RECALL ANYTHING QUITE SO FAIR AND PRECIOUS; UNLESS IT BE, PERHAPS, THE HEAD OF THAT SUPREMEST MASTERPIECE OF GREEK SCULPTCHAH, THE ILYSSUS, WHEREOF INDEED, IN A CERTAIN GRACIOUS MODELLING OF THE LOVELY NECK, AND IN THE SUBTLY DELECTABLE CURVES OF THE CHEEK AND CHIN, IT FAINTLY, YET MOST EXQUISITELY, REMINDS ME!"

Chorus of Fair Enthusiasts (who still believe in Prigsby). "OH, YES!—YES!—OF COURSE!—THE ILYSSUS!!—IN THE ELGIN MARBLES, YOU KNOW!!! How TRUE!!!!"

top Oscar Wilde dressed for the part. This photograph of him in his aesthetic lecturing costume was taken by Sarony of New York, who specialized in visiting celebrities.

above One aspect of aestheticism that most infuriated manly Philistines was the sexual appeal pretty girls found in sensitive intellectuals.

From New York he was to go to Philadelphia, Baltimore, and Washington. From Philadelphia he went to visit Walt Whitman. The two poets immediately established comfortably friendly relations: they each liked being on christian-name terms and they had each been accused of publishing immoral poetry, so they had a little in common. Their poetry, of course, could not have been more different, Whitman being one of the most truly original poets who ever wrote, and Wilde one of the most derivative of poetasters. But there was something of the flamboyant phoney in each, and they enjoyed posing before each other and the press as celebrities engaged in an historic meeting. Oscar even swallowed without a murmur Whitman's assertion that 'the fellow who makes a dead set at beauty itself is in a bad way'. A bottle of the old poet's home-made elderberry wine may have been still more unpalatable but Oscar was always kind and polite when treated kindly, and he professed to enjoy both the wine and the milk punch that followed it.

Baltimore missed its promised visit. Wilde was supposed to attend a reception there with Archibald Forbes, a British war correspondent who was also travelling Morse's lecture circuit. But Forbes, a professional lecturer, had picked up the topicality of Wilde's arrival and added a feeble joke about Aesthetic clothes to his lecture. Wilde heard about it, took umbrage, cut Forbes on the train to Baltimore, and rode straight on to Washington, thereby offending all the citizens of Baltimore who had expected to meet him. Morse was left with a tricky little quarrel to sort out. Forbes complained that Wilde had made insulting remarks about him to the press: Wilde claimed that he had been misreported, but demanded that Forbes stop sneering at holy art; Forbes refused to withdraw; Wilde turned on Morse, and claimed that incompetent secretarial advice had caused him to miss dinner in Baltimore. It took D'Oyly Carte himself to unruffle Morse's feathers and cajole an apology from Wilde. But it was altogether an unedifying incident.

Boston was the next city to hear the great lecture. This curious loop back supports Wilde's minor complaint against Morse that his tour had been planned with some disregard for geography. But Boston was the scene of an undoubted triumph. It had the strongest intellectual tradition in the United States and was disposed to regard European culture favourably. Wilde could hope for an intelligent and sympathetic audience.

To make sympathy doubly certain, he was lucky enough to be subjected to an abortive rag by some Harvard University students. The front rows of the Music Hall, where the lecture was given, were taken by sixty students, who dressed themselves in Bunthorne breeches and velvet jackets, and wilted languidly to their places, fussing foppishly over the sunflowers and lilies they carried, after the rest of the audience was seated. Wilde was forewarned, and wore ordinary evening dress to spike their guns on his appearance. He strengthened his position by accepting the joke with perfect good humour, and won complete victory when he mildly remarked, 'I am for the first time impelled to breathe a fervent prayer – Save me from my disciples!'

When Yale students foolishly tried to repeat the identical jape a week later in New Haven, Wilde could afford to ignore them entirely, and apart from a noisy and unfriendly audience in Rochester, New York, he was henceforth spared student demonstrations. But the demonstrations had been valuable to him. They embarrassed local pride, and compelled the press to treat him with apologetic courtesy. Wilde was sufficiently pleased with some of his triumphs to have copies of Philadelphia papers sent to a wide range of friends: Mrs Langtry,

Whistler, Edmund Yates, and Magdalen Junior Common Room among others. Whistler and his Tite Street friends responded with a typical telegram:

'Oscar! We of Tite Street and Beaufort Gardens joy in your triumphs, and delight in your success, but – we think that with the exception of your epigrams, you talk like Sidney Colvin in the Provinces, and that, with the exception of your knee-breeches, you dress like 'Arry Quilter.' Signed J. McNeill Whistler, Janey Campbell,
May Elden, Rennell Rodd.
New York papers please copy.
(Colvin and Quilter were the two art critics most despised by Whistler's set).

Rennell Rodd, a young poet with whom Wilde had visited France the previous year, was in the process of breaking off his friendship as it might stand in the way of a successful diplomatic career. Wilde went to some trouble to find a publisher for Rodd's poems in Philadelphia, and oversaw the production of a beautiful and Aesthetic limited edition, with engraved decorations and print in brown ink on transparent brown paper, interleaved with sheets of apple green. He wrote an introduction, and puffed the book, which would never have been published without the support of his name. But Rodd claimed to be mortally offended by Wilde's cheek in writing a florid dedication to – himself!

To
OSCAR WILDE
'HEART'S BROTHER'
These few Songs and many Songs to come

Rodd protested to the publisher that this was 'too effusive', and objected to being identified with 'much that I have no sympathy with' in the preface. Certainly Oscar Wilde was not the safest of associates for a young establishment careerist. There were too many doubtful questions. Even in New York one irritable old clubman had insisted upon calling him 'she', explaining away his obvious meaning with the feeble pun, 'I heard it was a Charlotte-Anne'

To the delight of the public that hoped Oscar would indeed prove a charlatan, the great Aesthete declared himself little more impressed by Niagara Falls than he had been by the Atlantic. The citizens of Chicago were less delighted when he criticised the ugliness of their toy-fort-like water tower. As it was the only edifice to have survived the great Chicago fire it was held in some esteem by Chicagoans, and Oscar forfeited popularity. But the Mid-West demanded sufficient lectures to necessitate the order of new breeches, stockings, and a velvet doublet from a theatrical costumier. And there were certain successes. In Minneapolis, a patriotic St Patrick's Day audience of Irishmen cheered a rousing nationalist oration from Speranza's son. From Keats's elderly niece in St Louis he received as a gift the manuscript of his idol's 'Sonnet on Blue'. It was framed and hung in a position of honour when he returned to England.

He struck west through Nebraska, and faced the four-day train journey to California. The Sierra Nevadas impressed him, though his sense of fun was unchecked, and he wrote home that he was 'somewhere in the middle of coyotes and cañons: one is a "ravine" and the other a "fox", I don't know which, but I think they change about'.

California turned out to be the loveliest part of America he had seen. He had become dispirited with the endless dun colouring of the eastern seaboard states in January and February, and found nothing of interest in early spring in the flat Mid-West. So that a return to a lush green countryside was an enormous fillip to his tired Irish spirit.

Better still, he found that his reception in San Francisco exceeded anything he had experienced elsewhere in the States. The West was used to long-haired men – vigorous fighting men, like Custer and the old frontier scouts. The West enjoyed his lecture; asked for more, and was given some suggestions for the improvement of American house decoration.

San Francisco provided, unexpectedly, the finest examples of good taste in the country. In the Chinese ghetto the artefacts and household goods of the poorest people were delicate and beautiful. In his lecture Wilde compared the Chinese labourer's teacup favourably with the gaudy dinnerware of luxury hotels. He anticipated the frosty tones of his own Lady Bracknell in his severities on landscaped pottery: 'We do not want a soup-plate whose bottom seems to vanish in the distance. One feels neither safe nor comfortable under such conditions.' And he urged Americans to be bolder in their use of colour for interior decoration, holding up Jimmy Whistler's famous Peacock Room – a rich and beautiful piece of design which had appalled the businessman who commissioned it – as 'the finest thing in colour and art decoration which the world has known since Correggio'.

He started his return eastwards on a more southerly route, passing through Utah and Colorado. The enormous Opera House at Salt Lake City, where he lectured to the Mormons, seemed to him supremely ugly. So did the Mormons themselves, though their President had one charming daughter. Polygamy seemed to Wilde prosaic, and the great Mormon Tabernacle was more like a soup-kettle than a building. It was with some relief that he left for Denver, where he found that the Rockies were the one feature of natural grandeur in America whose beauty had not been exaggerated.

left San Francisco in the 1870s.

left below Military correspondent Archibald Forbes disliked Oscar, and ridiculed aestheticism in his own lectures to American audiences.

below Julia Ward Howe, author of *The Battle Hymn of the Republic*, befriended and defended Wilde in Boston.

bottom New Haven Green and Yale University in the nineteenth century.

Denver was waiting excitedly for Wilde's visit. It was still essentially a silver mining town, although Austin Tabor, the dashing 'bonanza king', had just built a modern opera house there, to which Wilde would be the first important foreign visitor.

A substantial section of Denver's population was still made up of prostitutes who nominally served the miners, but actually enjoyed the enthusiastic protection and support of the city fathers as well. One brothel madam, with the delightfully apt name of Rose Lovejoy, prepared to greet Oscar by decorating her parlour after the Aesthetic fashion, so far as she understood it. At least she hung Japanese fans on the walls.

Two lively girls from a rival establishment ornamented their persons instead, and appeared in public wearing huge sunflower and lily hats over yellow dresses. When this finery attracted the dubious attention of a humourless policeman, one of them yelled at him, 'I know what makes a cat wild, but what makes Oscar...?' The constable's mind slowly tried to take this in, and he decided to arrest the girls for causing a public disturbance. When the red light district suggested that every whore in town would go into Aesthetic dress if this attempt to infringe their liberty continued, the charge was dropped. But the Denver press appealed to Oscar to come quickly and rescue his fallen disciples.

After this elaborate prelude, Oscar's arrival was almost anticlimactic. He was tired from travelling, and clearly didn't care much one way or the other whether ladies of the streets offered themselves as Aesthetes (though he denied that the sunflower was meretricious). He had been much more interested to discover on the train that his poems had been pirated in America, and were being sold cheap to travellers by small boys.

Leadville, the mining camp near Denver, was rougher and more exciting. Tabor, as Lieutenant-Governor of Colorado and owner of the biggest silver mine, took the English visitor out to see this genuinely Wild piece of the West. Oscar was lowered down a mineshaft in a bucket, drank a lot of whisky with the miners underground, inspected the street of squalid cribs that was Leadville's red light district, and thoroughly delighted this tough community by his unshockable capacity to take a hard night's drinking and sight-seeing in his stride.

His journey back east took him through St. Joseph, Missouri, where Jesse James had just been killed. Oscar was amused that a criminal should become a public hero, and even more amused by the frantic scramble of townspeople who tried to buy up the dreary suburban household goods that were now valuable as 'relics' of the bandit's domestic life. And on to Kansas, where a local poet insisted on reading the visitor his 3,000 line epic on the Civil War, with its great climax:
'Here Mayor Simpson battled bravely with his Fifteenth Kansas Cavalry.'

From the Mid-West Oscar struck north for Canada, and gave lectures in Ottawa, Montreal and Toronto. In the hope that he might earn enough money to pay for a year in Japan he accepted any further lectures Morse could arrange. This took him back to New England for some repeat performances, then down to the South through Georgia, and across the Gulf States to New Orleans and Texas.

Like most nineteenth-century Englishmen, Oscar Wilde enjoyed the South. People's manners were so much better and the pace of life was so much calmer than in the brash and bustling North. If the Western miners were the best dressed men in the country, their boots and corduroy breeches reminding Wilde of his beloved cavaliers, the southern belles were the most beautiful women in the land. Or at least, it did no one any harm to tell their local newspapers that they were.

In New Orleans Oscar went to see ex-slaves practising voodoo rites. He visited Beauvoir, to meet Jefferson Davis, the overthrown President of the defeated Confederacy. Rather tactlessly, Oscar rhapsodised to his Boston friend, Julia Ward Howe, about the 'beautiful, passionate, ruined South, the land of magnolias and music, of roses and romance': tactlessly, because Mrs Howe was the author of the *Battle Hymn of the Republic,* and so in herself quite a strong part of the force that had destroyed the slaving Confederacy. But Mrs Howe had publicly defended Oscar in Boston against a violent onslaught on the indecency of *Charmides,* so no doubt she was willing to allow a poet an unusually sensitive response to the South.

After his six-week southern tour, Oscar returned to the North-East, put away his lecture notes, and treated himself to a well-earned holiday at the millionaires' summer resort, Newport, Rhode Island. At this point he could congratulate himself on a well-spent six months. He had achieved more publicity than either he or D'Oyly Carte had anticipated. His tour had been a success: some people were calling it the greatest transatlantic lecture tour since Dickens's public readings. He had won friends wherever he had been, and had proved that he was capable of serious thought and serious argument. And he had earned more than a thousand pounds. Now all this was to be dissipated in five months' useless hanging around.

Wilde's first play, *Vera, or The Nihilists,* had been written in England and intended for production in 1881, with Mrs Bernard Beere in the title role. Unfortunately, in March 1881, Czar Alexander II was assassinated, and although interest in Russian subversive politics rose to such a peak that the Adelphi Theatre announced its intention of opening *Vera* in December, there were some doubts about Wilde's pro-revolutionary attitude. The royal family had no doubts at all: they did not wish to see a pro-regicide play which included an assassination on-stage mounted in the West End. Oscar was not willing to face the Prince of Wales's disapproval, so he agreed to *Vera's* being dropped in London, and hoped that he might persuade Marie Prescott to put on the play in New York. Failing that, he was keen to write another play, for the American actress Mary Anderson, whom he admired. And so he wasted the summer writing passages of blank verse for Mary Anderson's *The Duchess of Padua*, and trying to elicit a firm commitment to produce *Vera* from Marie Prescott. His novelty was worn out, and the press openly wondered why he did not go home.

In October Lillie Langtry came over to make her debut on the American stage. Oscar went down to meet her off the boat with a huge bunch of lilies, and of course he praised her loudly to the press. When her play opened he reviewed it, by special invitation. He praised her costumes and her beauty, and silently ignored her lack of talent. But not even the arrival of the Jersey Lily could persuade the press that there was any remaining interest in Oscar Wilde.

There would, no doubt, have been a good deal of interest, had it been widely known that the supercilious Oscar fell victim to a crude confidence trick. A young man in New York claimed to be the son of an acquaintance of Oscar's, and told a sad tale of his nervousness about collecting a lottery prize. Oscar kindly went with him, and found himself steered into a den of charming men, who frankly and freely paid the youth, and offered Oscar a friendly game to show there were no hard feelings... When Oscar left, with empty pockets, he began to wonder whether the original young man had been a victim or a bait, and he took this question to the police. He was able to identify the youth from police photographs, as a notorious 'bunco-steerer'. The police, for their part, were grateful to Wilde for coming forward and giving them the chance to press charges against the gang. Far too many victims of confidence tricks preferred losing their money to losing face, so that swindling throve for lack of evidence against swindlers.

At last, just after Christmas 1882, Oscar sailed back to England, taking with him the remains of his profits from the lecture tour, Mary Anderson's agreement that she would appear in *The Duchess of Padua* if it suited her when complete, and Marie Prescott's promise to try and produce *Vera* the following year.

Jefferson Davis, President of the Confederacy in the Civil War. After the defeat of the South he lived in retirement at Beauvoir, where he received Oscar Wilde.

below Mary Anderson, the American actress much admired by Wilde. He wrote *The Duchess of Padua* for her but the play did not please Miss Anderson and she never appeared in it.

MODEST FAILURE

'La poésie française a toujours été parmi mes maîtresses les plus adorées, et je serais très content de croire que parmi les pòetes de France je trouverai de véritables amis.'

Now was the time for Oscar Wilde to build on his American success, and confirm the serious reputation he was starting to make. Certainly he tried. After a short visit to London he went to Paris where he spent three months, hoping, presumably, to conquer another new society as he had conquered America.

He took with him *The Duchess of Padua* and worked hard at it, confident that Mary Anderson would finally accept it, and his rewards would be rich. But although hard work kept him from the opening of Jimmy Whistler's exhibition 'Arrangement in Yellow and White', where the favoured colour was extended as far as the artist's socks, Oscar still had to allow himself a little self-dramatisation and affectation. This took the form of a conscious imitation of Balzac. He took rooms in the Hôtel Voltaire which he filled with books by and about Balzac. A passage in which Balzac declares that constant labour is the law of art and life became his inspiration, and he would regret sitting over relaxed cafe meals with his friends, saying, 'I ought not to be doing this. I ought to be putting black upon white – black upon white.' In his rooms he kept flowers on his writing table at all times, and used a large porcelain bowl as an ashtray, for he was already a chainsmoker. In the later years of his domestic prosperity he might be encountered in the small hours of the morning, slipping downstairs in a dressing-gown to raid his own ashtrays for cigarette-ends, if he had permitted himself to run out of cigarettes before going to bed.

'The Oscar of the second period', as he now liked to call himself, imitated Balzac by wearing a great white dressing-gown with a monkish cowl while he wrote. Outside he carried an ivory cane with a turquoise handle, as the young Balzac had done. His hair was curled in exactly the style of a bust of the young Nero in the Louvre. But the breeches were abandoned for ever. Oscar wished to impress sophisticated Parisians, not the Philistine bourgeoisie.

It was unfortunate, therefore, that his beloved fur-collared overcoat gave the strongest possible impression of a bourgeois businessman in Paris. Combined with Oscar's Neronian hair-style, jewelled hands and semi-precious cane, it was more odd than effective. Oscar's wit, too, fell on somewhat unreceptive ears. He offered a vein of lightly mocking persiflage that could only have been understood and accepted by an audience acquainted with those attacks on 'Bunthorne' and 'Postlethwaite' which had led him to adopt a suspect pose, and then sustain and undermine it at the same time. As Shaw later noted he shared with Mark Twain, of all people, a taste for the tall story which assumed that the ideal listener detected his lie, and enjoyed its combination of the plausible with the preposterous. But some Parisian auditors were literal-minded: when he told old Edmond de Goncourt that the theatre in the Wild West used condemned murderers to play villains, so that Macbeth and Lady Macbeth might be duly killed on stage at the end of a performance, he was believed!

The grandest lion Wilde met at this time was Victor Hugo. The old master was accustomed to receive visitors in a formal double-row of armchairs. Wilde was honoured with the place next to Hugo's senior disciple. But no sooner had the English visitor started to dominate the company in an attempt to win Hugo's admiration than he was told, 'The master sleeps'. Wilde's wit had failed, and he was forced to carry on trying to entertain a gathering of fellow-courtiers in a respectful undertone.

Sarah Bernhardt was visited twice. Once at the Vaudeville Theatre where she was performing in one of Sardou's plays. She was changing her clothes when Wilde came into the dressing-room, but she stuck her head out through the curtained screens and greeted him ecstatically, to the jealous irritation of the handful of men already in the room. The second visit was to her house, where Oscar took an

A caricaturist's view of Oscar before and after his American trip, with a sadly ironic forecast.

OUR CAPTIOUS CRITIC.

Our Oscar as he was when we loaned him to America

YES, you can sound the trumpets and beat the drum (the big one). Our Oscar has returned, America has parted with the precious loan we made her, and Oscar is in dear happy England

once again. "Mr. Oscar Wilde's Lecture," I read on a little pale green, in fact, "greenery yallery," card, and further, on a dear, delightful, charming old handmade paper programme, rich with old type and bad grammar, I learnt that our Oscar had covered some 30,000 miles of transatlantic territory, and was about to give his "personal impressions" of the same at the Prince's Hall, Piccadilly. Ah! how I counted the days and hours until the time should arrive for the apostle of the true and beautiful to meander on to the platform and deliver himself of his luxurious platitudes. At last it came. But why should I rack my soul with the memory of my great disappointment? O, America! What have you been and gone and done? This was not the long-haired and attenuated æsthetic we sent you. These are not the knee breeches we swathed him in when we set him afloat on the disappointing Atlantic. O, you too too quite too practical world, you have broken the base of our hopes, you have almost washed out the scent of the roses of our dearest joy. In short, you have fattened our Oscar, you have cut his hair, and you have returned him (this side up without care) in a suit of very ordinary dress clothes and a last year's "masher collar." Not even his personal impressions can be taken as a return for this wanton destruction of our idol, though they were so replete with personality concerning himself. Still, there he stood, a bad imitation of the human creature he had so long girded his righteous soul against for being unlovely. Postlethwaite is on the wane and our own Oscar is about as gone a coon as you ever sent up a gum tree. Columbia, I am done with you; you have obliterated my star, and your stripes are heavy upon me. Let me be calm and consider the "lecture" which I heard the remnant of Oscar Wilde deliver at the Prince's Hall in Piccadilly. First there was his grand contempt for longitude and

Sure I just bought it because I knew it was Irish

The American lady who purchased our Oscar's tresses and "banged the chignon" with them

Frightful foreshadowing of our Oscar's future if he had not cut his hair

and, boarding the trim-built "Lady Tyler," float away to Dutchland, and settle down with pipe, beer, and saurkraut. (Should you do so, my dear Oscar, promise me one thing—that is, not to be disappointed with the sea; it is very mild and in-

Our Oscar as he appeared on being returned to us!

latitude, and his artless description of the Western World panting to receive him; "the interviewers" boarding his steamer in a storm miles from the American shore; then came the good old jokes, old and time-honoured, as the "Here we are again; how do you do to-morrow" of Mr. Merryman at Christmas, and given with an oleaginous unction (Delmonico has certainly ruined Oscar's figure) that could not fail to captivate the listener. Then there was the dash of poetical word-painting. The spoken panorama of the great continent, glowing with rich and subtle tints, brilliant as the picture on a tea tray ("one of these given away with every pound"); and later on we came to the vital point of the Postlethwaitian pilgrimage to the benighted land of Cousin Sam. "Now let us consider," said Oscar, assuming pose No. 32 in the "Shilling Guide to Deportment," "let us consider what I have done for America." What had he done? Well, at a protracted hour of a sweltering July evening he ran off a few advertisements for Buggins of Chicago and Juggins of Boston—hardware men whom he called "Artists in Iron," and compared with Cellini; finally he succumbed to the impatience of his hearers—who had come to scoff and remained to swear—and retired amidst an enthusiastic putting on of hats and mantles. I do not know what to say for the style of Oscar Mild's—I mean Wilde's—"lecture." Original it certainly was, to a degree. It chiefly consisted of a tautological use of the words and phrases, "Beautiful," "charming," "extremely," "seems," "seems to me," "pleasure of meeting," &c. The egotism of the deliverance was unbounded, especially in such passages as the following (Pose No. 15, "Shilling Guide to Deportment"): "I have seen (in America) crowds at theatres, sometimes at my own lectures, and sometimes at great public festivals." The style of delivery can, perhaps, be better culled from a quotation than from a lame attempt at description. Here you are then; now what do you think of the poet's prose?—*The whole scene I saw in the moonlight being the most fantastic scene I ever saw.* The hoigth of foine language entoirely, isn't it? So, farewell, Oscar; like Samson of old, your glory and strength have departed with your hair, and, I believe, should you remain amongst us, even the tax-collector will not accept a refusal on the plea of æstheticism. You are in a parlous state, good shepherd. Should you grow your hair again, you will have to take yourself to the Great Eastern Railway, book for Harwich,

Frightful foreshadowing of our Oscar's future should he continue to cut his hair and resume the knee breeches

offensive, compared with the Atlantic). Just one word more. Should you continue to cut your hair, for dear life do not resume the "*Patience* Advertisement Costume," or the result may prove too terrible

59

Paris in the second half of the 19th century. The Boulevard des Capucines.

above Edmond de Goncourt, diarist of the
Paris literary scene. An elderly man when he
met Wilde, he believed and recorded some of
his tall stories. From a lithograph by William
Rothenstein, 1894.

below Victor Hugo. A visit to the old master
was the high point of Wilde's stay in Paris,
but Oscar's wit failed to keep Hugo awake.

armful of wallflowers, much to her delight. This time it was he who behaved ungraciously. When a visiting French writer addressed him as *'Cher maître'* and treated him with great respect, Oscar only found him 'tedious'—his strongest word of condemnation at the time

The gossips of Paris were sure that the petite Baroness Deslandes was Wilde's mistress. He certainly spent a great deal of time sitting at her feet, and persuaded Burne-Jones to paint her. Goncourt, puzzled by the conflicting rumours, recorded in his journal that Oscar Wilde was a creature 'of doubtful sex'.

The poetry and example of Baudelaire now began to exert an influence on Wilde second only to that of Balzac. He followed the French poet's example of drinking absinthe, and was only inhibited in his wish to smoke hashish by its comparative inaccessability. Although he found two glasses of absinthe pleasant, and enjoyed picturing roses blooming in the dust of the streets, three glasses, Wilde observed, were unbearably prosaic: the drinker saw everything as it really was. And under such a vision of unsupported actuality, who could bear, say, a black silk top hat? In fact, there was never any real danger that he might become enslaved to drugs or drink: the weakness that was to destroy Wilde was intoxication with himself.

In this Baudelairian phase we should, perhaps, consider the term 'decadent' rather than 'Aesthetic'. Artistic decadence (a descriptive, and not a pejorative term) has been described as 'an intense self-consciousness, a restless curiosity, an over-subtilizing refinement upon refinement, a spiritual and moral perversity'. French poetry had given the lead in this. Gautier's *l'art pour l'art* had encouraged subtle refinement, and Baudelaire's discovery of 'flowers in evil' had developed curiosity and perversity. The painting of Toulouse-Lautrec during the decades when Oscar Wilde was associated with Paris provided a fine visual reflection of the spirit of decadent art. Baudelaire, for example, had first noted the disturbing mixture of squalor and eroticism in the sight of suspenders and stocking-tops against thighs. Lautrec painted just such momentary body-blows of decadent observation, including portraits of Oscar which ruthlessly exposed the ultimate corruption of his fastidious superiority.

With far less talent than his French masters, Wilde wrote poetry in the 1880s which might have modelled itself upon the text-book definition of decadence. The two poems upon which he was engaged in 1883 were *The Harlot's House*, and *The Sphinx*, a long piece which he had started in Oxford, and was not to publish for another ten years. *The Harlot's House* achieved its effect of 'spiritual and moral perversity'

Sarah Bernhardt, wearing her elegant trouser suit as she works on a self-portrait bust in her Paris studio.

right Balzac, by Rodin. Balzac was Wilde's literary idol during his first stay in Paris and Rodin's sculpture delighted him, both as a work of art and as an object which scandalized the middle-classes.

by juxtaposing an innocent pair of lovers walking home before dawn with the sounds of dancing in a brothel. For some quite unexplained reason the girl goes into the brothel, although she and her lover have previously agreed that its occupants are a mockery of life. Dawn beautifully breaks to give the poem a conclusion of saccharine artificiality. The rhythm is clumsy enough to be Speranza's own work, and the poem perhaps found its proper resting-place at those numerous occasions over the next few years when the poet was invited to recite it before Lady Wilde's hushed and respectful guests.

As a poet, Wilde was to make the acquaintance of other poets in Paris. He met Paul Verlaine, but found his ugliness repulsive. Verlaine, for his part, envied the constant stream of expensive cigarettes Wilde gave himself from his silver case, while the French Bohemian had to make do with cheap tobacco. A meeting with Mallarmé was more satisfactory, though Mallarmé's answer to the invitation to meet Oscar at lunch had been so ambiguous that no one knew for sure until he had arrived whether he would come or not. Novelists were slightly less friendly. Zola and Daudet both formed unfavourable impressions of the English dandy and Daudet, almost alone among French men of letters, was later to go so far as to rejoice at his downfall.

But if Wilde failed to make important friends among the established French writers, he was making himself known as a friend of France and of French culture. An English writer who knows and respects the French writing of his own day is always one of a minority. Such a writer, who also speaks French fluently, loves to visit France and pay his respect to the French *maîtres;* who shows by all he says and does that he understands the true value of an intellectual reputation in France; who can skip away from French anglophobia with the assurance that he is *Irlandais,* such a writer is, if he be at all talented, assured of achieving some continental success in the long run. Oscar Wilde was laying the foundations of that reputation abroad which still outweighs his honour in his own land.

From the point of view of his English reputation the most important friend he made in Paris was Robert Harborough Sherard. This dull young English journalist, a great-grandson of the poet Wordsworth, was not impressed by the celebrated Oscar Wilde when he met him at a friend's house, and went out of his way to be rude to him. With his normal tact and consideration Oscar closed his eyes and ears to insults, and affected to believe that Sherard had invented a striking and unusual pose of Philistinism. Within a few days he had charmed the young man into complete sympathy, and it was not

right Charles Baudelaire, the French poet who declared that poetry had no other end but itself – a statement which complemented Gautier's assertion that art was its own justification. Baudelaire's influence on Wilde was second only to that of Balzac.

far right Robert Harborough Sherard, whom Wilde met in Paris and who was determined to remain unimpressed. A dull young English journalist, Sherard later capitulated to Wilde's charm and became a loyal friend and compulsive biographer.

below Paul Verlaine, by C. Bacchi. His stormy life and career included a term of imprisonment but his poetry achieved greatness. When he met Wilde in the 1880s he envied the younger man his casual success.

long before Sherard had fallen into the hero-worshipping posture he was to adopt toward Wilde until his own death in 1943. In 1883, friendship with Sherard gained Oscar access to a few literary homes he might not otherwise have entered so early. Sixty years later, friendship with Wilde in the past was still the most important thing in Sherard's life, and he had written four books on the subject.

Sherard planned a volume of poems and Oscar offered him encouragement in those early days. He also asked Sherard to seek out obscure and precious words for inclusion in *The Sphinx*, and thanked him profusely for offering 'nenuphar'. (He was unable, however, to help with a trisyllabic rhyme for 'catafalque'). Sherard wondered why Oscar, with his extreme aversion to ugliness, tolerated him. Oscar assured him that he had 'the head of a Roman emperor of the decadence – the head of an emperor who ruled but for one day – a head found stamped upon a base coin'. A more serious bar to their friendship lay in the fact that Sherard lived at Passy, some way from the centre of Paris, and there kept dogs, which Wilde detested. So the two met to eat at expensive restaurants in the city centre, and Wilde assured his friend that the advance he expected from Mary Anderson for *The Duchess of Padua* justified any extravagance.

Alas, the advance never came. The play was completed in March, and sent to America with a long and carefully thought-out letter on its production possibilities. A curt telegram rejected it, and Wilde, with the greatest good humour, said nothing more than 'This is rather tedious, Robert' to the dashing of his hopes.

In the summer he had to return to England. His money was running out, and *The Duchess* had not refilled his purse. Still, he had discovered one talent in America, and he exploited it in England. He gave two public lectures. One, *The House Beautiful*, was a refurbished version of the advice on interior decoration he had given on his return through the States. The other was a delightfully witty, malicious, and exaggerated account of his impressions of America. And at last, in August 1883, he returned to New York, as Marie Prescott was definitely producing *Vera*, and lasting fame might be at hand.

He took great interest in the production details. He demanded one elaborate yellow set, and yellow uniforms for the Nihilists. Since the Czar's favourite decor was a yellow-hung room (according to the play) only Whistler could have felt that the great hue was not being overworked. Perhaps it was as a relief that Oscar insisted on a vermilion dress for the heroine in one late scene.

The play opened at the Union Square Theatre on

20 August and seemed a certain success after the second act. The author was called, and received an ovation. But there were two more acts to follow, including that in which Vera's costume as well as her words were to Wildean specification. These were a complete failure, and the evening ended in an uproar.

Marie Prescott had an enterprising idea which would have saved the play. She was willing to tour it if Oscar would play opposite her. But Oscar had acted one part across the States already in the cause of making his name. He now refused to put his dignity further at risk. So *Vera* closed after a short and unsuccessful run, and Oscar returned to England, where his stock had fallen a little in the course of 1883.

MARKING TIME

'I am afraid that writing to newspapers has a deteriorating influence on style. People get violent, and abusive, and lose all sense of proportion, when they enter that curious journalistic arena in which the race is always to the noisiest.'

To make a living Wilde had to continue lecturing. His principal topics remained 'The House Beautiful' and his American experiences, though as the years went by he was willing to vary this with general opinions on art, or special lectures on individual figures like Chatterton.

In Liverpool, a seventeen-year-old boy named Richard Gallienne was taken by his father to hear the speaker from London. Richard was entranced by the lecturer's fine, sensitive voice, and felt himself strongly drawn to the worship of beauty that the lecture proposed. Any trace of lingering Lancashire caution was blotted from his mind when his hard-headed businessman father confirmed that there was more sense than might have been expected in Oscar Wilde. Oscar had made a disciple who was to throw up his business career before it had begun, come adventurously to London, and propose for himself the life of a poet and man of letters. With his name poetically extended to le Gallienne, Richard was to become a leading figure in *avant-garde* circles in the nineties, and the closest imitator of the young Wilde that the 'Professor of Aesthetics' ever had. Le Gallienne adopted a velvet jacket and flowing tie as normal wear, and posed in breeches and a Tennysonian 'poet's hat' in the woods. Oscar privately laughed at this 'cycling costume', but with his good figure and finely-chiselled photogenic face, le Gallienne became the very figure of the representative poet of the age of *The Yellow Book*. He lived until the 1940s, almost forgotten in England, although he continued to write, and one of his two remarkably handsome daughters became a well-known actress. But in the 1880s he was simply an unknown young man with a rather conventional taste for poetry who was one of the many recipients of Oscar Wilde's encouragement and kindness.

Perhaps the adulation of sensitive adolescents was the more important to Wilde at this time as he was, in fact if not in feeling, a journalist. Oscar the Artist despised journalism, and launched many unfriendly sneers at its practitioners. But a journalist he was himself in the early 1880s, and grateful to find the work. He reviewed poetry in the *Pall Mall Gazette*; he wrote arty gossip for the *Court and Society Review*; he took over Willie's theatre column in the *Saturday Review* when his brother was on holiday.

Artistic self-importance ensured that he took a high and lofty tone when writing letters to the press; he still wrote as though he had been sent down from Parnassus to correct the faults of inferior writers. But it seems likely that he made enemies at this time by that same high tone. For all his personal charm and amiability, he could not hope to retain the friendship of his fellow-journalists if he insisted on asserting his own superiority to their common calling. And in fact, almost the only journalists who remained friendly and proved it by their loyalty in adversity ten years later were those who, like Frank Harris and Bernard Shaw, also felt themselves to be above the common run of Fleet Street. Years after Wilde's death, Shaw pointed out that even his mode of friendliness had been unsuited to the world of the press. Wilde liked to be called 'Oscar' by his friends and 'Mr Wilde' by his acquaintances. But Fleet Street had for years rubbed along in the simple democratic cameraderie of unadorned surnames for everyone. Wilde embarrassed men by insisting that an exception be made in his case.

The ridiculous peak of his career as a journalist came in 1887, when he was invited to become editor of the *Lady's World* at a salary of six guineas a week. The superior artist was only too glad to accept, though his sense of linguistic decorum quite properly compelled him to persuade the publishers to alter the title to *Woman's World*. This was a trivial job with trivial pay, but he was by now a married man with two children and he needed the security it offered.

Oscar Wilde was an appropriate choice of editor

for a women's magazine. His early publicity-seeking had been conducted under the illumination of stage and society beauties with whom he was still on friendly terms. He was a lecturer on and possessor of a 'House Beautiful', for he had bought No. 16 Tite Street, and decorated it in ways that were known to be the very last word in tasteful fashion. He had always shown himself obsessed with clothes. From the publisher's point of view there was nothing incongruous about asking him to step down from the springs of Helicon to the boudoir basin.

He turned out to be a surprisingly conscientious editor. It was the first time he had held a position of authority and responsibility within an established organisation, and he responded well. He wrote to a wide range of fashionable and intellectual ladies, soliciting articles. Some refused: there were to be no contributions from Julia Ward Howe, or Ellen Terry's sister Kate; and Sarah Bernhardt, although she allowed her fashionable tea-gown to be featured, did not offer her own thoughts on the subject. Bold in the cause of duty, Oscar even wrote to Queen Victoria, asking if Her Majesty had written any early verses that might be reprinted. Predictably, that prosaic monarch had never in her life written '*one line* of *poetry* serious or comic', and in a hoity-toity minute she dismissed the request as based on '*invention* & a *myth*'.

But work was received from royalty. H.R.H. Princess Christian contributed a piece on nursing, and Queen Elizabeth of Roumania, using her pseudonym, 'Carmen Sylva' was happy to write for Oscar. An assortment of Countesses and Honourables kept the social tone high enough to suit the editor's and readers' snobbery. Lady Archie Campbell was among the old friends who put in a piece, and Speranza, offering herself now as Lady Wilde, was back in fine form with a piece of bombast about *Historic Women*:

> Yes, they have lived! those women whose
>   great names
> Are graven deep on the world's history:
> Strong, splendid souls that chafed at
>   human wrong...
> And tyranny, and servile servitude.

On the whole, though, the *Woman's World* printed work by an unusually distinguished selection of contributors during Oscar's two years as editor, and can probably compare favourably with any women's magazine ever, over a comparable period of time. Posthumous work from Mrs Craik, the author of *John Halifax, Gentleman*, was accompanied by a tribute to her. Thackeray's daughter, Mrs Ritchie, had a small literary reputation in her own right, and contributed. Ouida, the popular novelist, sent in a

Richard le Gallienne, young poet, protégé, and imitator of Oscar Wilde.

No. 16 Tite Street, Chelsea; the exterior of Oscar's 'House Beautiful'. The house was built in the 1860s.

Fleet Street in the late nineteenth century. Though he earned
his living by journalism for a number of years Wilde was never
at home there, and few journalists had any liking for him.

right *The Woman's World* for August 1888.

piece: Oscar was later to give her discreet financial aid when her public deserted her. Olive Schreiner and Edith Simcox made more lasting reputations. Arthur Symons and Violet Fane came from Oscar's own decadent and Aesthetic circles.

The editor himself contributed notes on literature and fashion. His literary notes were almost unfailingly kind – indeed, over-generous. On fashion he made the interesting prediction: 'It is . . . probable . . . that the dress of the twentieth century will emphasise distinctions of occupation, not distinctions of sex.' And this veiled prophecy of rational uni-sex clothing was not the only way in which he showed himself something of a Women's Liberationist. An essay bluntly called 'The Position of Women' was much needed in 1888, and it was supported by pieces like 'The Fallacy of the Equality of Women', 'The Fallacy of the Superiority of Men', and, a real challenge to Victorian sexual exclusivism, 'Women and Club Life'. It was not for nothing that Oscar, when putting the works of John Stuart Mill on his list of books that no one should ever read, excluded the *Essay on Liberty*: the great Victorian feminist had an unexpected follower in the *fin-de-siècle* hostesses' delight.

The editor of *Woman's World* was responsible for its illustrations as well as its text. He wanted to get away from the dull succession of fashion-plates that made the magazines of the day look, to his eye, like clothing catalogues. Under Oscar Wilde, *Woman's World* featured a great many full or double-page lithographs by rising artists. Bernard Partridge, the leading cartoonist of *Punch* after Tenniel, contributed light decorative panels after the Japanese style. Other painters who were to be the leaders of Art Nouveau in England contributed to this far from arty journal. Ricketts and Shannon, the amiable pair who devised covers and decorations for Oscar's books in the 1890s, sent in work. Walter Crane, the leading exponent of Art Nouveau before Aubrey Beardsley, produced a characteristic full-page for Beatrice Crane's 'Legend of the Blush-Roses'. Only one essential name was missing: Whistler's.

By the end of the decade Oscar and Jimmy had quarrelled irrevocably. Whistler acknowledged that 'his nature needed enemies', and that for him friendship was only 'a stage on the way to a quarrel'. Friendship with Oscar lasted until 1885. By then Whistler felt that the pupil was making too much of the master's ideas, and showing insufficient humility to the master. Oscar had once asked directly for his help with a lecture on aesthetics, yet in that lecture tiresome men like Ruskin and Pater were held up as the proponents of ideas, and Whistler was only presented as the exemplary artist.

In 1885, Whistler set out to challenge Oscar on his own ground. He gave a 'Lecture at Ten O'Clock' in the Prince's Hall, London. Here he put forward his own ideas with his own wit, but perhaps with less humour and clarity than they were accustomed to receive from Oscar. Oscar reported the occasion for the *Pall Mall Gazette*. He praised Whistler's 'really marvellous eloquence'. But he also called him 'a miniature Mephistopheles, mocking the majority', which was, perhaps, tactless from a tall man to a short man. And he finally trailed his own coat by asserting roundly that the poet and not the painter was the supreme artist. Whistler was put out, and responded characteristically with a barbed letter in *The World*, suggesting that Oscar chose his exemplary painter-theoreticians rather ill. Oscar evidently thought that this was to be another light-hearted public exchange, and sent a reply in keeping:

'Dear Butterfly, By the aid of a biographical dictionary I discovered that there were once two painters called Benjamin West and Paul Delaroche, who recklessly took to lecturing on Art.

As of their works nothing at all remains, I conclude that they explained themselves away. Be warned in time, James, and remain, as I do, incomprehensible: to be great is to be misunderstood. *Tout à vous*

OSCAR.'

But Whistler was in no mood for an exchange without ill feeling. He returned to unprovoked public attack two years later, linking Oscar's name with that of the despised barrister art-critic, 'Arry Quilter, and accusing his former protégé of plagiarism:

'What has Oscar in common with Art? Except that he dines at our tables and picks from our platters the plums for the pudding he peddles in the

provinces. Oscar – the amiable, irresponsible, esurient Oscar – with no more sense of a picture than the fit of a coat, has the courage of the opinions – of others.'

Longwindedness sometimes blunted Whistler's sting. Oscar was briefer, and his good humour was evidently strained:

'Atlas, this is very sad! With our James "vulgarity begins at home," and should be allowed to stay there.'

Whistler allowed this to rankle for four years, and then in 1890 took advantage of an article on plagiarism in *Truth* to return to the attack. He wrote a long, silky letter, complaining that Oscar had not been mentioned, and harked back six years to the original lecture Oscar had given after unacknowledged Whistlerian coaching. He allied himself with a disgruntled travel-writer named Herbert Vivian, who had been sweetly turned down by Oscar when he asked him to write an introduction for one of his books. In revenge, Vivian published hostile stories about Oscar, one of which seemed to vulgarise an incident in the Wildes' family life. Oscar sprang to the defence of his wife and children, and reprimanded Vivian in no uncertain terms. Vivian sulked for so many years that he lived to be the only man who ever snubbed Vyvyan Holland for being the son of Oscar Wilde. He was not the happiest of allies for Whistler to choose, and this may explain why Oscar adopted a tone of lofty pomposity, instead of the cutting banter which was the only stylish response to Whistler's motto, 'Who breaks a butterfly upon a wheel?'

'It is a trouble for any gentleman to have to notice the lucubrations of so ill-bred and ignorant a person as Mr Whistler,' Oscar told the editor of *Truth*, and the exchange marked the final curtain on their friendly relations.

Whistler had found a new connoisseur-disciple in Robert de Montesquiou, the prince of the Paris Aesthetes. He exchanged malicious gossip with him about Oscar's unaesthetic experiment in pipe-smoking. Montesquiou always disliked Wilde: he may have envied the Englishman's friendship with Sarah Bernhardt, who had once been his own mistress. And he always disliked in others that flamboyant appearance of aesthetic homosexuality for which he himself was notorious. For him Oscar Wilde was 'The Antinous of the horrible'. Wilde was not given to disliking people, even when they harmed him. But Jimmy Whistler had declared himself an enemy, and there was nothing to be done about it.

For one lost friend, Oscar felt he was making many new ones. It was in the late 1880s that he really began to build up his position as a great diner-out. Like Mahaffy he adored being seen at the tables of

below left Frank Harris in 1895, from a painting by William Rothenstein. A bounder, a liar, and a braggart Harris was nevertheless a brilliant editor, and proved a loyal and generous friend to Oscar Wilde.

below 'Had Shakespeare asked me...' Max Beerbohm was provoked to draw this wickedly funny comment on Harris in 1896, after hearing the subject declare that, while he knew nothing of the joys of 'unnatural' vice, he would have felt bound to submit '... had Shakespeare asked me'.

bottom Bernard Shaw, like Wilde, was an Irishman in London. The two were not close friends, but encouraged each other's early plays, and Shaw learned much from Wilde about the use of witty dialogue.

the titled, and like Mahaffy he made sure that his charm and wit earned him a welcome. His capacity to win over hostile parties was remarkable. It was only to be expected that ladies should enjoy his company: he and they shared household interests in common. But there was no obvious link between Wilde and Matthew Arnold's 'Barbarians' – the upper-class sportsmen who saw life from the saddle of a horse. It was Oscar who characterised the English fox-hunting gentleman as 'the unspeakable in full pursuit of the uneatable'. Yet at weekends in the great country-houses, where the unspeakables gathered in force to massacre grouse, Oscar charmed away their suspicions and made himself the life and soul of their parties. Numerous bluff, anti-Aesthetic gentlemen, who took their opinion of Wilde and all his works from *Punch*, went away from a first meeting convinced that he was not such a bad fellow after all.

These social successes led Oscar to believe that he was making his way up the steep Victorian class ladder, and becoming an intimate of the aristocracy. The Prince of Wales had long condescended to know him slightly, but then the prince was a notorious democrat, who was willing to count Jewish financiers among his friends. The old county families in their old country houses constituted a far more charmed circle that was far more difficult to break into.

By the time he was spending weekends with the Duke of Newcastle at Clumber, Oscar felt he had established himself among the leaders of English society. He was disastrously wrong. For the most part they regarded him as no more one of themselves than their servants. Cards sent out inviting ladies and gentlemen to dinner 'To meet Mr Oscar Wilde' might seem very impressive if the host and hostess were a duke and duchess. But they reduced Mr Wilde almost to the level of a society entertainer. When the crisis came, Oscar's aristocratic 'friends' dropped him completely and ruthlessly. He was an outsider, and his fate was of no interest to them.

It was as a diner-out that he first met that other great outsider of the 1880s and nineties, Frank Harris. Five foot five inches tall, barrel-chested, possessed of an enormous bass voice and an immense black moustache, aggressive, self-confident, adventurous, Harris was one of the most unusual figures ever to appear in the world of letters, and a most unlikely friend for Oscar Wilde.

Like Wilde, Harris was a noted conversationalist. But his method of dominating a table was to shout down all competition, and then fill the room with booming boasts and lies. He was perhaps the most prodigious liar English literary society has ever seen: Oscar and Speranza were models of truthful and decorous restraint by comparison. Yet there was no need for Harris to glamorise his life so fancifully: it had, in all conscience, been far more adventurous than most. He had run away to America as a youth, and there worked as a labourer excavating the foundations of the Brooklyn Bridge, as a hotel clerk in Chicago, and as a cowboy. He had passed a short time acquiring some education in Lawrence, Kansas, and then got himself posted to Russia as a war correspondent. Returning slowly to England through Europe, he studied at both Heidelberg and Göttingen universities. Then he began his swift climb through Fleet Street, editing first the *Evening News,* then the *Fortnightly Review*, and finally buying control of the *Saturday Review.*

He was a brilliant and daring editor. He turned the *Evening News* into a successful cheap paper with Conservative politics by printing stories whose sensationalism ultimately led to his dismissal. He sacked the august roster of distinguished dons, lawyers and clergymen who had made the *Saturday Review* a pillar of the establishment, and encouraged the brilliant young talents: Shaw and Wells, Max Beerbohm and Symons. Poetry and fiction came from Hardy and Kipling: wit from Wilde.

Readers of the *Saturday Review* were kept well-informed about new artistic movements: decadence, impressionism, early post-impressionism, Ibsenism. No such successful and adventurous editing was seen until Ford Madox Ford took over the *English Review* a decade later.

Wilde admired Harris's skill as an editor, and the two found that a conversational relationship was quite possible, provided both talked brilliantly at once, and neither attempted to listen to the other. Fearless Frank, who astonishingly managed to avoid public scandal himself, despite his constant womanising and outspoken sexual boasting, was to prove a loyal friend when scandal engulfed Oscar.

The last two decades of the nineteenth century were proving a great age of scandal. Intolerably restrictive social conventions made the fall into public disrepute easy, and recovery well-nigh impossible. Charles Stuart Parnell and Charles Dilke saw their political careers founder on accusations of adultery. Oscar's old enemy Lady Colin Campbell lost her social position after she and her husband had flung mud unsuccessfully at each other in a sensational divorce petition. A member of the Prince of Wales's set was utterly disgraced for cheating at cards during a weekend party at Tranby Croft. The investigation of a male brothel in Cleveland Street led a rich aristocrat into self-imposed exile. The times were ripe for a really resounding scandal. The actual imprisonment of a distinguished public man would provide a perfect ending to the reign of Mrs Grundy.

Oscar Wilde joins the fashionable audience at a scandalous trial: the first Parnell case, when it was proved that an attempt to link the Irish Nationalist leader with political murders in Dublin rested on mere forgery. But Parnell's adulterous liaison with Mrs Kitty O'Shea was later used to end his career.

Mr. Parnell points out his signature in the Kilmainham Prison-Book

Mr. F. C. Macdonald, Manager of the "Times," gives evidence as to the purchase of the letters

Mr. Soames, Solicitor to the "Times"

Mr. Woollacott, a Central News Reporter who gave evidence as to Mr. Parnell's explanation of his signature

The Duchess of St. Alban's and Mrs. Adair listen to the cross-examination of Mr. Soames

Mr. Oscar Wilde, Mr. J. L. Toole, Mr. Conyns Carr, and Mr. H. Beerbohm Tree are spectators of the Commission drama

SIR CHARLES RUSSELL CROSS-EXAMINING MR. SOAMES

Sir Charles Russell: "Did Mr. Pigott inform you that he had told Mr. Lewis he himself had forged the letters?"—Mr. Soames: "He told me he had told Mr. Lewis nothing of the kind. He told me Mr. Lewis endeavoured to get him to say so." Sir Charles Russell: "Then he told you he had told Mr. Lewis he had not forged the letters?"—Mr. Soames: "He did." Sir Charles Russell: "Tell us, please, what he said?"—Mr. Soames: "He showed me a letter, signed by Mr. Lewis, accusing him of having admitted that he had forged them, and his reply. On that I required a statutory declaration to be made, and on that you will find he relates all that passed between himself and Mr. Lewis, including the offer of £1,000 by Mr. Labouchere to get in the witness-box and say he forged them." (Great sensation)

73

FAMILY LIFE and SINISTER SOCIETY

'When one is in love one begins by deceiving oneself. And one ends by deceiving others. That is what the world calls a romance.'

In 1883, a lecture tour took Oscar Wilde to Dublin. Among many visits to be made in the city of his birth, one was to a fairly recent acquaintance. Constance Lloyd, '...a beautiful girl...a grave, slight, violet-eyed little Artemis, with great coils of heavy brown hair which make her flower-like head droop like a blossom', as Wilde told Lillie Langtry, had met him in 1881 at her home in London. She had found him surprisingly pleasant: 'never a bit affected' when talking to her alone. Now, at her grandmother's in Dublin, he was not so pleasant: 'decidedly extra affected' when he called. His lecture was disappointing. He went to dinner at Trinity and missed Miss Lloyd's theatre poetry. Altogether the renewed acquaintance was rather a let-down. It was quite ridiculous that Miss Lloyd's nearest and dearest should tease her about Oscar Wilde.

And yet...*Vera* did seem very fine when she read it...and Oscar's explanation of the play was ever so impressive, if a bit hard to understand...and...in short, within three days Miss Lloyd was engaged to marry Mr Wilde.

She was the daughter of an Irish barrister who had died in 1874 after doing very little for his family. Her brother Otho had gone up to Oxford while Oscar was there, at which time Speranza had asked her son to look out for him. Constance had inherited a small private income, and had reasonable expectations of inheriting a good deal more from her grandfather, whose successful career had included a fellowship at Brasenose, membership of Parliament, and a lucrative spell as a railway lawyer. The old man was known to be dying, but, as Willie Wilde noted with amusement, the news of his grand-daughter's marriage revived him, and he took a new lease of life.

Willie's stories might well have a faintly malicious tinge when he talked of Oscar. The elder brother's journalistic career appeared reasonably successful during the 1880s yet he knew that he had

disappointed his mother's hopes. She knew him for an erratic boozer, who took from her money she could ill afford, and sponged off others.

Oscar, by contrast, still held out hope. When earning, he tactfully left small presents of money on Speranza's mantelpiece. His life seemed well-ordered, and he still had time to enter some established profession. 'Take warning by Willie,' Speranza wrote when her younger son seemed to be drifting uncertainly on literary journalistic tides. But with marriage in prospect, and a small assured income from Constance, she could plan an ideal future for him.

'I would like you to have a small house in London and live the literary life and teach Constance to correct proofs, and eventually go into Parliament,' she told him.

The literary life of course came. Parliament was a vain hope. The 'small house' was to have a fame of its own. But first there was the wedding.

On 29 May 1884 Oscar Wilde married Constance Lloyd at St James's Church, Sussex Gardens, Paddington. The ceremony was of the kind that the bridegroom regarded as 'quite private'–that is to say a considerable crowd attended, but they were largely uninvited spectators attracted by the show. Whistler, still a friend at this date, sent one of his best telegrams to arrive just before the service. 'Am detained,' it read. 'Don't wait.'

The crowd had plenty to look at. The bride's dress and veil were of aesthetic shades of cowslip and saffron. It was said that the striking silver girdle she wore was the groom's present to her. It was not known whether the myrtle leaves which composed a wreath for her hair and liberally decked her dress had been suggested by the groom's wreath-loving mother.

The bridesmaids were still more striking. Two infants led the way, wearing long dark red silk dresses with yellow sashes. Red and yellow feathers waved in their big picture-hats. At their throats were amber necklaces and bunches of yellow roses. In their long yellow gloves, each held a bouquet of

below Oscar Wilde at the age of twenty-eight. From a drawing dated 1882.

bottom Constance Lloyd, whom Oscar met in Dublin in 1883. They were married in London a year later.

white lilies. The four grown-up bridesmaids wore similar costumes, with the addition of pale blue over-dresses and knots of red ribbons among the feathers in their hats.

The only guest who could compete with this spectacle was a lady who was described as wearing a 'very aesthetic costume'. This was a red silk underdress covered by a red plush smock, and a white lace hat trimmed over the crown and under the brim with red roses. It has been suggested that this vision of red and white was probably Speranza.

Oscar's own appearance was relatively muted, but no one could have mistaken the wedding as the work of any but the great clothes-reformer. The ladies' dresses all conformed to one of his cardinal rules: they hung in straight Grecian folds from the shoulders, and were not gathered in at the waist or hips for the addition of bustles or crinolines.

After the reception, the young couple (he was nearly thirty, and she was three years younger) left from Charing Cross for a honeymoon in Paris. There they went to the opera, to art exhibitions, and, naturally, to see Sarah Bernhardt. She was playing in *Macbeth* during their stay, and the production impressed Constance hugely: 'only Donalbain was bad.... Sarah of course superb, she simply stormed the part'.

A few days after their arrival Sherard came to breakfast with them in their hotel. He was charmed with Constance, who seemed to him 'supremely happy'. The bright, sunlit hotel room 'was full of flowers and youth and laughter'. The whole thing seemed intolerably cheerful in Sherard's morose eyes, and he handed over his swordstick to Oscar, lest he be tempted to despatch so unnaturally happy a man. Constance kept the swordstick, and later joked with him about it.

After the visit, Sherard walked out into the morning sunshine with Oscar, and was impressed when his friend stopped at the nearest flower stall, and sent a bouquet back to the wife he had just left. He was startled, as well he might be, when Oscar turned the conversation to the delirious delights he had experienced in the marital bed with Constance. But he was not in the least surprised when, later in the honeymoon, Oscar announced that 'The criminal classes have always had a wonderful attraction for me,' and left Constance alone while he and Sherard toured the most squalid slums of Paris, ending in a room where diseased drunks sprawled over the floor like corpses.

On their return to England, Oscar and Constance took lodgings, while Godwin and Whistler supervised the decoration and refurbishing of No. 16 Tite Street for them. A newspaper had called Constance 'the châtelaine of the House Beautiful', and Oscar was now putting her money to work to create the perfect interior he wanted.

The dining room was in shades of white, with 'each table a sonnet in ivory, and the table . . . a masterpiece in pearl'. He wrote to Godwin, 'we find that a rose leaf can be laid on the ivory table without scratching it – at least a white one can'.

Constance's drawing room had a background of white and cream. Against this, faded brocades were hung, and engravings and etchings, including a number of Whistler's, adorned two walls. A large copper relief by a young sculptor Oscar had encouraged in Chicago hung over the fireplace, and a portrait of the master of the house by Harper Pennington hung opposite. Two peacock's feathers were let into the ceiling – this was on Whistler's insistence.

Oscar had two studies. Upstairs, a large room decorated with the lavish red and gold he loved, held his books and, eccentrically, his bath. The furniture there was oriental: divans and rugs encouraged lounging and sprawling. But his actual writing was done in a little room on the ground floor just beyond the front door. Here he had placed Carlyle's writing desk, which he had acquired. Around it, the walls were buttercup yellow, picked out with red lacquer. On a red lacquer stand in the corner rested a cast of the Hermes of Praxiteles. And on the wall there were a Japanese print, a Monticello, and a drawing by the disreputable, drunken, homosexual Aesthete, Simeon Solomon.

In this house the master and mistress were framed before the world as the young couple of perfect taste. Constance dressed according to Oscar's rules, and he showed off his home and his wife alike to the admiring world. And the world noted with pleasure and satisfaction that the graceful young couple were very much in love.

At first the two were separated, as they had been during their engagement, by Oscar's lecture tours around Britain. But once settled employment came with the *Woman's World* there was no such need for Oscar to be away from home and he ceased writing poetic, loving letters deploring the fate which took him to Scotland while she was in London. The letters themselves marked a move in the direction of economy: to his betrothed, Oscar had sent daily telegrams whose open affection (he hoped) astonished the clerks.

But affection was fast dying down, unhappily, and in some dangerous ways. In 1885 the Wildes' acquaintance Henry Labouchère, a Radical MP, added a sinister amendment to an otherwise innocuous Criminal Justice Act. On 5 June that same year Constance gave birth to a son. Oscar was delighted. But the proud father had already ended

below Willie and Oscar Wilde: Oscar and Willie Wilde. The grossness implied here had a basis in fact; but it might be said that Max Beerbohm's caricature is also guilty of grossness.

right and bottom Paris in the late nineteenth century: Les Halles (right) and New Year's Day on the boulevards (below). Robert Sherard, in the city when the Wildes arrived for the honeymoon, was not surprised to find Oscar willing to neglect Constance while he indulged his fascination with Paris street-life.

his public act as a proud husband. Pregnancy had ruined the effect of Grecian folds in Constance's clothes, and when she could not be shown off as an object of beauty Oscar began accepting dinner invitations without her.

She was not deeply missed. Constance was a limited woman, content to take Aesthetic opinions from Oscar, and with little of her own to contribute to artistic circles. Her private beliefs were remote from the Aesthetes' joyous Paterian paganism: she approved of evangelical missionary efforts, and could not understand her husband's flippant belief that missionaries were divinely ordained food for starving cannibals. Nor was she the perfect housekeeper for a sybaritic husband: at dinner one day Oscar wearily put down the carvers after trying to cut a chicken she had sent up, and said, 'Constance, why do you give me these—pedestrians—to eat?'

He was usually polite and deferential to his wife. He refused other people's invitations for Wednesdays, when she entertained. But he was almost transparently bored by the company she invited. Equally, his own friends expected a dull interlude if they called and found that Constance was to entertain them while they awaited Oscar.

After the birth of his second son Vyvyan, in 1886, his affection was lavished on the boys. As they grew older Cyril, at least, became aware that his mother was not always happy. When Oscar, with his usual gentle kindness, tried to do his duty as a Victorian papa and asked his sons what they thought happened to little boys who were naughty and made mother cry, one of the children boldly asked him what punishments were reserved for 'naughty papas, who did not come home till the early morning and made mother cry far more'.

It was hard on Constance. She was doing her best to act the part of her brilliant husband's wife. She contributed pieces to the *Woman's World* on muffs, and children's clothes. But even these revealed a simple, commonsensical soul, much concerned with necessary warmth, and opposed to the absurdities of white satin for grubby children. An afterthought of loathing for the tartan velvet encouraged by Queen Victoria sounds as though her editor-husband might have inspired it. Constance found her false reputation as a fashion expert embarrassing.

She tried to write a children's book. It created no stir. As Oscar's fame mounted in the 1890s she made one final effort, and prepared a volume of *Oscariana*. Oscar disapproved of her selection, and predicted that the book would be a failure.

Worst of all, perhaps, the sexual ecstasies Oscar had described to Sherard were increasingly being shared with young men instead of Constance. As early as November 1885 Oscar heard from a

above Mrs Oscar Wilde – her husband's showpiece at a charity occasion.

above right The Hermes of Praxiteles. A cast of this famous marble graced a corner of Oscar's study in Tite Street.

right The interior of the Cafe Royal, from a painting by Charles Ginner.

Cambridge undergraduate who had been a Salisbury Street neighbour five years earlier. Always indulgent to the young, Oscar was quite willing to entertain the lad and discuss art with him. When Harry Marrillier did come to tea, conversation quickly moved in an intense direction that was not quite what du Maurier's caricatured Aesthetes had meant by 'intense'. From Newcastle, where he had to give a lecture, Oscar penned a cry of regret that Harry had let him catch his train. They should, he said, have gone together to the National Gallery to look at 'Velasquez's pale evil king, at Titian's Bacchus with the velvet panthers', and at Fra Angelico's heaven. Perhaps in an afterlife Oscar might become a flower – a red geranium, for his sins? And a sinister Oxford word recurred: his hour of conversation with Harry had been 'intensely dramatic and intensely psychological'.

For a few months, at least, Oscar kept the young man suspended as a possible lover. He asked him to write, yet wrote himself as though their affair were over. He told him 'that there is no such thing as a romantic experience', yet lured him with the promise of 'a land full of strange flowers and subtle perfumes . . . a land where all things are perfect and poisonous'. Altogether it was a masterly seduction of sensitive adolescence, made possible because Oscar was totally sincere in his own adolescent conviction that beautiful exotic, 'strange sins' existed. His mature intellectual recognition that 'there is no such thing as a new experience at all' was not to become emotionally ingested as a profound conviction until he had endured the, for him new, experience of suffering.

It was during the following year that Oscar Wilde met Robert Baldwin Ross. 'Bobbie', as he was known at this date, was then seventeen. The son of an Attorney-General of Canada, he had been brought to England at the age of two, on his father's death. He was preparing to go up to Cambridge within a few years. And he was, by all accounts, richly experienced in homosexual practice by 1886.

Bobbie's career at Cambridge was short-lived. He quickly made a name at King's as an outspoken Aesthete. His writings in college journals annoyed the dons, and his artiness irritated the hearties. In spite of rowing for the college second boat, he suffered the fate normally reserved for the effete (or coxes) and was thrown into the college fountain. This led to his contracting pneumonia, and he left Cambridge within a year of going up. For the remainder of his life he was a literary journalist and art connoisseur in London. And he became an enthusiastic member of the inner circle around Oscar Wilde, reading and praising his work as it was written. Ross was convinced that his friend was a

truly great writer. And Ross was to prove himself unreservedly loyal, at some risk to himself. But to envious heterosexual outsiders, he seemed like a leader among a pack of perverted jackals, determined that their leader and their views should lead the art world.

But Oscar Wilde was not to be betrayed by lovers of his own class, even if they felt as jealous as Bobbie was to do when the time came for newer and younger men to replace him. By the end of the 1880s Wilde had discovered his true taste: he loved the excitement of pursuing the uneducated, the suggestion of depravity about the undisguised male prostitute, the anti-social cheek of the pretty boy who would let a rich mark do anything he liked for a good meal and a few quid.

Between Mayfair and Soho, the Café Royal and Kettners, fashionable drawing rooms and dimly-lit male brothels, Oscar Wilde led a titillating double life. In the Café Royal he entertained and was entertained by writers and artists. He became a notable figure, evoking admiration and envy. But pretty young undergraduate poets might be asked to come on from Mayfair to Soho; to drink 'red and yellow wines' at Kettners. And their friendship with Oscar Wilde might become even more intimate, in small private dining rooms. At the very least they were likely to become aware of the coarse, illiterate boys who also enjoyed Oscar's hospitality, and who were given silver cigarette cases, inscribed from their friend Oscar, in return for unnamed services rendered. 'Feasting with panthers' was Wilde's romantic description of mingling with the dangerously unstable potential blackmailers of the criminal homosexual underworld.

Will Rothenstein sober: Max Beerbohm, Charles Conder and Oscar Wilde drunk, at the Cafe Royal. Recalled by Rothenstein and drawn by Beerbohm.

LITERARY SUCCESSES

'All art is quite useless.'

By 1889 the editor of the *Women's World* was bored with his job. The excitement of rounding up contributors had worn off. The daily routine of travelling by the underground from Chelsea to the Strand had become so wearisome that it was no longer practised daily. The prohibition laid down by the publishers on smoking in the office had always been a heavy penance. It became intolerable. And so, confident that the stories and essays he had been publishing elsewhere were about to produce great benefits, Oscar Wilde resigned.

Over the next six years he published almost the entire corpus of literary work on which his serious reputation rests; 1889 to 1891 were the great years of Wildean essays and fiction. 1892 to 1895 saw him in his true métier as a dramatist. Only *The Ballad of Reading Gaol* and *De Profundis* are important works falling outside the enchanted years.

The first of Wilde's fugitive pieces to be gathered into book form were the fairy stories collected as *The Happy Prince and Other Tales*. The volume, illustrated by Walter Crane, appeared in 1889 before Wilde had actually left *Woman's World*.
Mr Gladstone, who by now was the involuntary owner of the nucleus for a collection of Wildeana, received his complimentary copy. A few months later the Grand Old Man declined to head the list of sponsors seeking a small pension from the Royal Literary Fund for Speranza, and he was given no more of Wilde's first editions. Ruskin was slow in acknowledging his copy. But Pater was quick to cheer his pupil with an enthusiastic letter, full of praise for the 'little poems in prose' to be found in the stories.

Polished and Paterian indeed was the prose of the first two tales. The remaining three were simpler, and reviewers were right to point to the influence of Hans Andersen on the volume as a whole. But in some ways the stories were unlike Andersen's. Andersen had accepted the division between rich and poor as inevitable; after the manner of a folk tale,

An illustration by Walter Crane for
The Happy Prince and Other Tales.
right Two story headings by Charles Shannon
from *A House of Pomegranates,* the collected
volume of Wilde's short stories which was
published in 1891.

THE BIRTHDAY ♣ ♣ OF THE INFANTA.

IT was the birthday of the Infanta. She was just twelve years of age, and the sun was shining brightly in the gardens of the palace.

Although she was a real Princess and the Infanta of Spain, she had only one birthday every year, just like the children of quite poor people, so it was naturally a matter of great importance to the whole country that she should have a really fine day for the occasion. And a really fine day it certainly was. The tall striped tulips stood straight up upon

27

THE YOVNG KING ♣ ♣ ♣

IT was the night before the day fixed for his coronation, and the young King was sitting alone in his beautiful chamber. His courtiers had all taken their leave of him, bowing their heads to the ground, according to the ceremonious usage of the day, and had retired to the Great Hall of the Palace, to receive a few last lessons from the Professor

B I

he used it to create pathetic sympathy for the poor, expose the follies of authority, and offer the satisfaction of the poor man winning the hand of the princess. Wilde, by comparison, rages about the inequalities of society. Poverty becomes the highest truth known to the Happy Prince: 'More marvellous than anything is the suffering of men and women,' he says. 'There is no Mystery so great as Misery.'

In another surprising way his tales are not only unlike Andersen's but remote from everything that he was himself supposed to stand for. Wilde shared Andersen's preference for a pathetic conclusion but instead of offering it as pathos for its own sake, a recognition of inevitable transcience, or punitive retribution, he chose to use it as a tragic pinnacle of noble self-destruction; a romantic acceptance of death as a nobler form of existence. Thus the Happy Prince and the swallow sacrifice themselves to the poor; the nightingale kills herself to further the love of others; and the Selfish Giant dies so that the Christ-child may receive him into Paradise. And, as no critics recognised, this was an amazing reversal of the hedonistic paganism Oscar Wilde was supposed to represent. The Pre-Raphaelite strand of medievalism which had always been a part of Aestheticism came to the fore; the Christian view that after-life matters more than life was stressed; and Wilde, the apostle of beauty, launched the most savage attack on the ethic which set beauty above all other values. 'As he is no longer beautiful he is no longer useful,' says the Art Professor, once the Happy Prince has given away his jewelled eyes and gold-leaf covering. And the Professor is being vehemently satirised; for in the eyes of God the most precious things in the city are the ugly cracked lead heart of the statue, and the dead bird who has helped strip it for the poor.

In the fairy tales that Wilde wrote over the next three years—(they were collected in 1891 and published as *The House of Pomegranates*)—the tendencies apparent in *The Happy Prince* became still more marked. The rich Paterian prose became universal, so that it was necessary for the author to tell a reviewer that the collection was not for children: 'I had about as much intention of pleasing the British child as I had of pleasing the British public.' The book was an elaborately beautiful object, designed by Ricketts with illustrations by Shannon. It was Art Nouveau in so *avant-garde* a form that some of Shannon's illustrations were barely visible: the new process they employed had failed.

But the stories themselves repeatedly attacked the worship of beauty. *The Young King*, who adores his newly-found splendour, perceives that it is based on the labour of the poor and the sufferings of

81

slaves, and refuses to wear his coronation robes. The hideous dwarf who dances at *The Birthday of the Infanta* dies of a broken heart on discovering that the Infanta has laughed at him out of contempt, and not loving admiration, and the Infanta (wickedly, we infer) demands that people with hearts be excluded from her presence. *The Fisherman and his Soul* part company that he may wed the soulless mermaid, and only his love for her saves him from the terrible corruptions his soul discovers in the appealing qualities of wisdom, prosperity and beauty. *The Star-Child* has to lose his beauty and suffer the kinds of cruelty he has inflicted on others before he can inherit his kingdom.

Hatred of cruelty runs through the stories like a backbone. Linked to it is an obsessive anxiety that the enjoyment of luxury and beauty may in itself engender heartless cruelty. Love and pity are elevated and enthroned.

Certainly, as Wilde's critical essays showed, his opinions at this time were undergoing change. But for two reasons it was very difficult to pin down exactly what he did think. In the first place, his generation admired paradox excessively. Wilde explained their position well: 'The way of paradox is the way of truth,' he wrote. 'To test Reality we must see it on the tight-rope. When the Verities become acrobats we can judge them.' But of course, when a wit of genius builds his critical theory around paradox it is difficult to know how much of the criticism is verity and how much is acrobatics.

And to make matters more difficult, it was undoubtedly one of Wilde's permanent canons that a concern for sincerity in artistic matters is misplaced. He was quite right to believe that the Victorian public placed too high a value on 'sincerity', and tended to ask of a writer, 'Does he mean it?' as if this were a more important question than 'Is it true?' But Wilde carried impudent 'insincerity' to an extreme. What can one do with a critic who disarmingly writes: 'Not that I agree with everything I have said in this essay. There is much with which I entirely disagree. The essay simply represents an artistic standpoint, and in aesthetic criticism attitude is everything.'

After that one cannot assert that 'Wilde believed...' a paraphrase of the essay. And yet it would be a fatuous (or perhaps over-scrupulously biographical) exercise to try and sort out the parts with which he 'entirely disagreed'. It is only possible to submit: to recount what the critic has said, treating it with proper detachment as a theory and not the expression of a personality, even though, paradoxically, the personality of Oscar Wilde leaps out of every phrase.

Briefly, the critical theories put forward in the

volume of essays called *Intentions* (1891) may be summarised as follows:

Art is not dependent upon nature; it is not an imitation of life. In many respects the pleasures it offers are greater than those found in life and nature. Therefore it is absurd to criticise works of art adversely for being unnatural or unlifelike. Realism is a mode without critical justification. The artist should be imaginative and creative; his work should be as far removed from mundane life as possible, and indeed the whole cultural ambience would be improved if people had more respect for beauty, splendour and the exotic, and less for scientific truth. But the artist is not the man who does most to preserve art in society. The critic is an indispensable middleman. The artist may perceive beauties that no one else has ever perceived in nature, but this very novelty of vision means that his work will be quite incomprehensible unless a man of equal talent can perceive his work as he does, and then communicate to the public the nature of the experience offered. The artist should restrict himself to questions of technique when discussing art: it is only the critic, the connoisseur who has trained himself to enjoy an endless succession of works of art, who will have anything to say about the experience they offer.

These really quite sober critical opinions were hard for earnest Victorians to take seriously. It was not that they feared, as many twentieth-century critics would, the 'escapism' of an art that deliberately transcends common experience (though to dismiss Wilde's thought on such a charge, as is sometimes done today, is little more than name-calling). What perplexed Wilde's contemporaries, and still keeps his ideas out of the mainstream of critical discussion, was the form of the two major essays. *The Decay of Lying* and *The Critic as Artist* both take the form of witty dialogues. Now there is a long tradition of dialogue as a vehicle for critical discussion. But respected precedents like Dryden's *Essay of Dramatic Poesy* gave little licence to the critic to employ wit in his dialogue, and certainly gave no hint of delightful distractions from the main topic like the following:

GILBERT: But I see that the moon is hiding behind a sulphur-coloured cloud. Out of a tawny mane or drift she gleams like a lion's eye.... There is nothing left for me now but the divine μονόχρονος ἡδονή [momentary pleasure] of another cigarette. Cigarettes have at least the charm of leaving one unsatisfied.

ERNEST: Try one of mine. They are rather good, I get them direct from Cairo. The only use of our *attachés* is that they supply their friends with excellent tobacco. And as the moon has hidden herself, let us talk a little longer.

The two essays that harmed Wilde most, however, were not included in *Intentions*. *The Portrait of Mr. W. H.* appeared in *Blackwood's Magazine*. It developed an idea that Wilde had discussed with Ross, and argued that the 'onlie begetter' to whom Shakespeare's sonnets were dedicated might have been a boy actor, with a name like 'Willie Hughes'. The essay took the form of a short story, in which a forged painting of the actor was used to overcome the problem that there was no evidence of Hughes' existence. The important argument put forward by the piece was the speculative suggestion that the early sonnets, in which Shakespeare urges a young man to marry and have children, were really urging the young actor to create new roles and serve his profession. There was no intrinsic reason for this to be found objectionable, but Oscar Wilde's reputation was somewhat dubious, and furious journalists hinted that this essay made the scandalous suggestion that Shakespeare had pederastic tendencies. It did not, although the sonnets and plays do. But Wilde suffered the storm of vituperation which always descends on those who point out this obvious fact, regardless.

The attack which Wilde found most distressing appeared in the Scottish *National Observer*. Its editor, W. E. Henley, had received favourable reviews of his poetry from Oscar, although his aggressive, colloquial, ballad-like style was not obviously to the Aesthete's taste. For a short time the two were friends, but when the aggressive, lame, Tory poet moved to Scotland to take up his editorship his normal quarrelsomeness asserted itself. Immersed in provincial Tory journalism, Henley found himself less and less able to tolerate the metropolitan broadmindedness Wilde represented. Wilde always took his acrimonious abuse seriously, for he did respect Henley's poetry.

There was some consolation in the presentation by Ricketts and Shannon of a charming imitation of an Elizabethan miniature in a perfectly faked frame, purporting to be the original 'portrait of Mr W.H.' Wilde was delighted, and it joined the other pictures in his study.

The Soul of Man under Socialism, published in 1891, did him less overt harm with the literary world. But it caused the society ladies and gentlemen he had charmed at dinner-tables to regard him with renewed suspicion. Socialism was an alarming word in the nineteenth century.

Of course, Wilde's interest in Socialism was, on the whole, apolitical. He was concerned about the health of the arts, and more than half his essay is concerned with the rather unsocialistic argument that the duty of every man is individual self-perfection, and the truest artist is he who is most

W. E. Henley, the lame, defiant conservative poet, whose friendship with Wilde did not last long. The sculpture is by Rodin.

truly himself. Socialism appears, almost casually, as a means to produce this desirable individualism, as the successful reorganisation of society on healthier lines would remove the tiresome distraction of having to care about the poverty of others.

This does not mean, as has sometimes been suggested, that Wilde did not know what Socialism was. On the contrary, he shows a very precise understanding of the political system he advocates:

'Socialism, Communism, or whatever one chooses to call it, by converting private property into public wealth, and substituting co-operation for competition, will restore society to its proper condition of a thoroughly healthy organism, and ensure the material well-being of each member of the community.'

And as long as he is discussing Socialism he is wonderfully free from the compromising apologetics by which some Fabians and Morrisites maintained their ties with the property-owning classes. Wilde enjoys shocking the bourgeoisie with paradoxical Socialist truths, and in the process, shows Shaw a way of conveying hard political ideas without inducing boredom:

'To recommend thrift to the poor is both grotesque and insulting. It is like advising a man who is starving to eat less. For a town or country labourer to practise thrift would be absolutely immoral.

The best among the poor are never grateful. They are ungrateful, discontented, disobedient, and rebellious. They are quite right to be so.

As for the virtuous poor, one can pity them, of course, but one cannot possibly admire them. They have made private terms with the enemy, and sold their birthright for very bad pottage.

What is said by great employers of labour against agitators is unquestionably true. Agitators are a set of interfering, meddling people, who come down to some perfectly contented class of the community and sow the seeds of discontent among them. That is the reason why agitators are so absolutely necessary.'

The man who held those views was certainly entitled to call himself a Socialist. But he was unlikely to be accepted as such by others, because it was all so unimportant to him. Socialism? Communism? What did the name matter to Oscar? He could never have joined earnestly in the factious splintering that the politics of the left was already making its own.

And if he held out no compromising sympathy to bourgeois prejudices, he was equally uncompromising with the dictatorial left. Authoritarianism was so great an evil that Wilde made no bones about preferring the continuation of hodge-podge capitalism, poverty and all. At least under the capitalist free-for-all *some* men were able to acquire great wealth, and thence, in a few cases, liberation of the personality, freed from financial concerns. And without totally free, whole men, Wilde saw no joy in society at all. He even disliked democracy if it meant the imposition of the will of an unliberated majority. Socialism might harness technology to alleviate drudgery and redistribute wealth equally, thereby freeing men from the need to conform to predetermined social patterns simply to acquire the means of existence. But if Socialism imposed conformity for its own sake it would stifle the arts and spirit of mankind. The soul of man under Wildean Socialism would be an individualist soul: in a current cant phrase, Wilde might be said to have looked forward to the opportunity for every one to 'do his own thing'.

The culminating triumph of the years 1888–1891 was the publication of the novel *The Picture of Dorian Gray*, first as a serial in *Lippincott's Magazine*, and then as an ornate volume designed by Ricketts. This was Wilde's most ambitious project to date, and he took it very seriously. Scurrilous attacks by Henley and his henchman Charles Whibley were answered politely. Praise in a review by Pater was most welcome when it came. But Wilde was beset by Philistines, proclaiming that he had written an immoral book.

The charge was even more absurd than is usually the case when self-appointed censors abuse a work of art. *The Picture of Dorian Gray* continues the astonishing anti-aesthetic trend that we have noted in the fairy tales, and which had received a further covert impetus from the *Intentions* essay 'Pen, Pencil and Poison'–a study of Thomas Griffiths Wainewright, murderer, forger, and minor literary figure, in which Wilde reduced *ad absurdum* the doctrine that art's values were paramount. His irony in the essay was missed by the public, as was the

quite severe moralising in *Dorian Gray*.

Dorian's delight in his own beauty and youth (symbolically shown to be transient through the portrait which ages while he remains untouched by time) leads him to place the stimulation of the senses through exotic beauty above every other value. This leads to his appalling corruption–symbolically exposed as he ages instantaneously at the moment of death, while his portrait returns to his innocent youth. The apparently innocent artist, Basil Hallward, is destroyed because he too has placed too high a value on surface beauty. And the witty idler Lord Henry Wotton, whose epigrammatic dialogue led critics to identify him with Wilde, is actually an aesthete with the true heartlessness of Whistler, too self-centred to care when his wife has deserted him; too self-satisfied to be anything but damaging to Dorian, and the more dangerous for his cold charm.

Wilde's novel made an assertion that should have silenced its censors for good and all, by showing that he agreed with the central tenet of censorship: 'Dorian Gray,' he wrote, 'had been poisoned by a book. There were moments when he looked on evil simply as a mode through which he could realize his conception of the beautiful.'

But the prurient and cruel were unable to appreciate the horror with which Wilde depicted this moral destruction of a young aesthete. The fact that he dared to talk about corruption was enough for them. And their unbalanced moral judgement emerged when they protested, not that Dorian Gray was shown to be a murderer and a blackmailer, but that it was distantly hinted that he might have been homosexual! In fact, Wilde made far more overt comments on the catalogue of heterosexual seductions and desertions among Dorian's crimes, but Henley and the Puritans were following the perverse moralist's usual course and criticising an author's reputation instead of his book.

The final absurdity was that Wilde adopted the stance his book had implicitly rejected. He added twenty-four aphorisms as a preface, designed to offend Puritanism as much as possible by the lofty assertion that form outweighs morality in works of art:

There is no such thing as a moral or an immoral book. Books are well written or badly written. That is all.

No artist has ethical sympathies. An ethical sympathy in an artist is an unpardonable mannerism of style.

Vice and virtue are to the artist materials for an art.

All Wilde's propositions were interesting and arguable. But his own practice defied them.

YEARS of TRIUMPH

'I took the drama, the most objective form known to art, and made it as personal a mode of expression as the lyric or the sonnet, at the same time that I widened its range and enriched its characterisation.'

The author of *The Picture of Dorian Gray* was decidedly somebody in the literary world. He had at least a nodding acquaintance with the writers of his own age – Henry James, Kipling, George Moore (who envied and disliked him, but was compelled to admit the charm of his company). He shared the universal respect for George Meredith. But he followed his own epigrammatic maxim, and always tried to learn from those younger than himself. So it was that Oscar Wilde became the mentor of the young poets of the 1890s who banded themselves together into the Rhymers' Club.

The club met more or less regularly at the Cheshire Cheese. Its members smoked churchwarden pipes, drank reasonably heavily, and read out their poems to each other. Twice they assembled their best recent work into an anthology. The Rhymers' Club was, on the surface, a jovial revival of an idealised Mermaid Tavern attitude to poetry: beautiful writing to be enjoyed by vigorous and merry young men.

Underneath things were different. The member who was to become truly great was W. B. Yeats. At this time, he, like Oscar Wilde and other Aesthetes, was beginning to realize the importance of William Blake. But Yeats was also messing around with sillier and more sinister ideas. He was, for a time, a member of an occult group led by the great charlatan Aleister Crowley – himself an overlush poet at this period. Without the stiffening of Irish politics, it is quite possible that Yeats' lyrical talent might have deteriorated into the vagaries of superstitious mumbo-jumbo, and he might have fallen to writing the sub-Shelleyan prating that passed for poetry among occultists.

Of the other members, only Richard le Gallienne outlived Yeats. He was mentally and morally robust by the standards of his fellow Rhymers, in spite of a

W. B. Yeats, like Oscar Wilde an Irish Protestant, made the most lasting reputation of all the poets of the 1890s. From a lithograph by William Rothenstein, 1898.

right The Cheshire Cheese, where the Rhymers' Club met in the 1890s.

lifelong tendency to sentimental womanising. But, alas, even at this time his talent was not equal to his appearance. As an apparently representative figure of the nineties, he does nothing to enhance the decade's reputation for literary excellence.

The two young poets whose brilliant promise ought to have developed to make their generation seem great rather than curious actually contributed more than any one else to the sense of the Rhymers as a 'lost generation'. Ernest Dowson and Lionel Johnson had real talent. Johnson was, in addition, a fine classical scholar. But both led undisciplined lives, and burned themselves out by the end of the decade. Thanks to them, and to the more simply unfortunate Aubrey Beardsley, the 1890s has the reputation of a decade of brilliant but doomed young artists, sailing close to the wind in their work, and pushing themselves right over into the pit in their private lives, until drink, drugs or dissipation led them to early death. Clearly Oscar Wilde was an appropriate symbolic patron for these young men.

At first Oscar's dearest friend among the Rhymers was John Gray, a handsome young man whom

Oscar, naturally, nicknamed 'Dorian'. He had a rival for the love of this young poet: André Raffalovich, a Russian emigre, who wrote poetry himself, and was jealous of Wilde's success. He had heard Oscar's casual dismissal of his ambition to play the literary host: 'André came to England to found a salon, but he only succeeded in starting a saloon.' And this rankled. He could not easily compete with Wilde for Gray's attention, but he was rich, and if Wilde was willing to pay the costs of Gray's volume of poems, *Silverpoints*, Raffalovich would be ready to open his purse when the time came.

When Wilde's attention was distracted by Lord Alfred Douglas, Raffalovich pounced. He followed Gray into the Church of Rome, and took him off to Scotland, where Gray became a successful parish priest and Raffalovich, his wealthy and devoted parishioner, built a church for him and dined almost daily at the presbytery. After Wilde's death, Raffalovich published a vindictive memoir of his former rival, packed with self-deceptive moralising.

It was in 1891 that Lionel Johnson introduced the fatal friend who was to wreck Oscar's life. Johnson was so small and fresh-faced that until the day when drink overwhelmed him, and he was found dead outside his favourite pub, he looked like an innocent schoolboy. His career at Winchester and Oxford was brilliant although, like Oscar, he found mathematics a sore trial. At school and college he was friendly with the handsome young aristocrat Lord Alfred Douglas. Douglas, too, was a poet; he worked hard at perfecting somewhat conventional sonnets. And it was as a young Oxford poet that Johnson introduced him to Wilde. Wilde was typically pleased to meet a member of the ancient Douglas family, but beyond sending the young man a handsomely inscribed copy of *Dorian Gray* he did nothing to extend the acquaintance for a year.

Instead, he went to Paris for another triumphal visit. Edmond de Goncourt's journal for the previous decade was by then appearing, and it reported Wilde as having said that Swinburne deliberately affected to practise the most monstrous vices. This had to be disputed, and in a dignified (if doubtfully honest) letter to the press, Oscar apologised for the inaccuracy of his French, which must have misled the old man.

There were new young friends to be made among the intellectuals of Paris. Pierre Louÿs, an intimate of the young and still unknown Colette, wrote elaborate, rather erotic poetry after Wilde's own heart, and, more surreptitiously, scandalous pornography which would probably have disgusted the Irishman. Louÿs addressed Oscar as '*Cher maître*' – always a delight for British writers.

Marcel Schwob was another young writer who

greatly admired the visitor from London, and sent him stories he had written that clearly showed the influence of *The House of Pomegranates*. A meeting with Marcel Proust was less successful. Proust invited the great man to dinner, but was unfortunately a little late himself. He arrived to find that Wilde detested the ugliness of his house (as Montesquiou had done before him), and had barely been polite to Marcel's parents, who were there to greet him. Wilde complained that he had expected a private meeting, and refused to stay for the meal. Success was leading to a dangerous high-handedness in his manner.

For an old friend, Oscar planned a new work. He would return to his early ambition, the drama, and create something splendid for Sarah Bernhardt. She should be a gorgeous and decadent *Salome*. Maurice Maeterlinck, the Belgian playwright, had devised a style of simple, repetitive, somewhat Biblical French, which could be imitated by a foreign writer whose command of the language was imperfect. And Louÿs, Schwob, and the young American poet Stuart Merrill, who wrote in French, all undertook to read the play and correct Oscar's grammatical slips.

Back in London, Oscar discussed the designs for the play with the artist W. Graham Robertson – ('What do you allow your friends to call you? "W"? or "Graham"?' he asked). The author's hope was that every character should be dressed in some shade of yellow, and braziers of perfume and incense should replace the orchestra. Ricketts, more cautiously, advised a black floor, a blue sky, and blood-red costumes for Herod and Herodias. Sarah, with French thrift, was determined to use the expensive costumes she had in stock from her Paris production of *Cléopâtre*.

But all was in vain. Rehearsals were under way at the Palace Theatre when the Lord Chamberlain stepped in and banned the production, on the ground that Biblical characters could not be represented on the English stage.

Oscar was furious. In an ill-judged moment of temper he announced that he would leave England and take out French citizenship. A delighted press pointed out that he would, in that case, face conscription. *Punch* drew him in the uniform of a *poilu*. And the idea was allowed to drop.

The setback was not really serious. By the time the plans for a London production of *Salome* had fallen through Oscar Wilde had already proved that he was a brilliant and successful playwright. George Alexander, the actor-manager, had been pestering him for a play for some time. Oscar satisfied him with the script of *Lady Windermere's Fan*, a melodramatic society piece lightened with drawing

room comedy; just such a play as Alexander was best fitted to produce. Alexander had been for years a member of Irving's stock company, and as such had been required not to outshine 'the governor' When he branched out on his own, the habit of restrained under-acting remained with him, and made him the leading exponent of realistic 'well-made' dramas.

Lady Windermere's Fan was, according to its author, 'one of those modern drawing-room plays with pink lampshades'. It was also a great success. Alexander had recognized a money-maker in the manuscript, and offered Wilde £1,000 for his rights in it. Wilde cannily trusted Alexander's judgement, refused, and made a larger sum from the play's run.

The old skill at self-advertisement was called in for the first night. One of the actors was given a green carnation in his button-hole. Oscar and several friends wore similar flowers, to create a minor sensation (It would have created still more of a sensation had Londoners known that the unnatural flower was the badge of the Paris homosexual). Oscar's speech to the audience after the final curtain became famous in its own right:

'Ladies and Gentlemen,' he said, 'I have enjoyed this evening immensely. The actors have given us a charming rendering of a delightful play, and your appreciation has been most intelligent. I congratulate you on the great success of your performance, which persuades me that you think almost as highly of the play as I do myself.'

In spite of this high opinion, he rapidly made some alterations for which the experienced Alexander had been pressing without success during rehearsals, and thereby improved the play considerably.

Only Bernard Shaw and William Archer gave the first night favourable reviews. The other critics were incensed by Oscar's impudent speech, and berated his ill manners in holding a cigarette while he delivered it. They claimed, not without justice, that the plot was secondhand and implausible: with less conviction they asserted that the passages of sparkling epigrams were of no dramatic value, and could easily have been composed by any second-rate talent. 'As far as I can ascertain,' Shaw commented drily, 'I am the only person in London who cannot sit down and write an Oscar Wilde play at will.'

The public loved it. Disregarding critical hostility, they flocked to the St James's Theatre. And although *Lady Windermere's Fan* (like *A Woman of No Importance* and *An Ideal Husband*) now looks more stagey and dated than Oscar's uncritical admirers like to admit, it was undoubtedly the most exciting new play by a British writer to appear since Sheridan.

In this year of triumph, Oscar Wilde received a

plea for help from Oxford. Lord Alfred Douglas was in trouble. Since the passage of Labouchère's amendment forbidding indecent acts between males, rich homosexuals had been ripe prey for blackmailers. The quaint old statutes, such as Henry VIII's degree of suitably Tudor penalties for 'the abominable crime of buggery' had been quite satisfactory for controlling the activities of professional male prostitutes and curbing public indecency. But nobody had thought seriously of using them against gentlemen, unless they were leading lives of such flagrant and felonious immorality that the charge of corrupting their servants might be added to a long list of other crimes. But now there was a simple, modern threat of two years hard labour for any convicted homosexual, no matter how discreet and harmless his way of life. And the indiscreet quickly found themselves at the mercy of 'renters' who sold their bodies first, and then, at higher cost and over a longer period of time, their silence.

When young Bosie Douglas (the name was a corruption of his childhood nickname, 'Boysie') came up to Oxford, he was already familiar with the sex life of a public school. He found that the intimacies with friends to which he had been restricted at Winchester could now be extended to a wider circle at university, and before long his habitual carelessness and indiscretion had put him in the hands of renters. None of his fellow undergraduates had the experience to cope with the situation. He was on bad terms with his father, the famous Marquess of Queensberry, who had given boxing its Queensberry Rules, and he could not expect help from that ferocious old heterosexual rakehell. He adored his mother, and did not wish to distress her with his difficulties. And so Oscar Wilde, the influential frequenter of gay circles in Oxford and London seemed a perfect sympathiser to help sort out the trouble. Wilde was quite willing to pass the matter on to Sir George Lewis, society's fashionable solicitor, who knew perfectly well how to handle these little imbroglios with discretion.

A year later, Max Beerbohm, in a private letter to Reggie Turner, gave a wonderful sketch of the kind of entanglements the law created for Oscar's circle:

'Bobbie Ross has returned to this country for a few days and of him there have been very great and intimate scandals and almost, if not quite, warrants.... I must not disclose anything... but I may tell you that a schoolboy with wonderful eyes, Bosie, Bobbie, a furious father, George Lewis, a headmaster (who is now blackmailing Bobbie), St John Wontner, Calais, Dover, Oscar Browning, Oscar, Dover, Calais, intercepted letters, private detectives, Calais, Dover and returned cigarette-cases

were some of the ingredients of the dreadful episode.... The... schoolboy Helen... was the same as him of whom I told you that he had been stolen from Bobbie by Bosie and kept at the Albermarle Hotel.'

Wontner, like Lewis, was a solicitor, but unlike Lewis he acted for the Metropolitan Police. Oscar Browning was a former schoolmaster who left Eton under a cloud, and was then given a fellowship at King's College, Cambridge, where he met Ross. Beerbohm's account suggests that the two Oscars again had to step in to rescue their young friends from a scrape.

But although little more than kindness may have led Oscar to intervene in 1892 the results were disastrous for him. He fell in love with Bosie. Soon he was writing to Ross that Bosie 'is quite like a narcissus – so white and gold... he lies like a hyacinth on the sofa, and I worship him. You dear boy....' It never occurred to Oscar, whose nature was utterly free from jealousy, that the 'dear boy' might

Blake's *Death on a Pale Horse*. The prophetic poetry and flowing graphic work of William Blake influenced nineteenth-century art from the Pre-Raphaelites to the Decadents.

resent the beautiful young aristocrat who had supplanted him in the great man's affections.

Superficially there was no reason to anticipate trouble from Oscar's falling in love with a cultivated young man. But Bosie was not like Bobbie. He was not in love with Oscar, and did not even have Bobbie's extravagant admiration for him. Of course, he was grateful to the man who had helped him out of a scrape, and like most of the artistic Oxford undergraduates, he admired the successful writer who had set the Aesthetic tone of student life. But Bosie was an aristocrat of aristocrats – it was part of his attraction for Oscar, who said, absurdly, that the name 'Lord Alfred Douglas' reminded him of a beautiful flower. And as an aristocrat Bosie found Oscar rather middle-class; perhaps a little vulgar. As Oscar was a leading light of those intellectual circles (almost entirely composed of middle-class writers and painters) for whom 'middle-class' was an insulting term, there was matter for discord here. For Bosie was arrogant, and did not conceal his contempt for some of Oscar's attitudes and turns of speech. To the son of a Marquess in a family of ancient nobility, Sir William Wilde's knighthood was very small beer, and Bosie was amused to hear Oscar solecistically refer to Speranza as 'her ladyship' when he thought he could get away with it. He twitted Oscar, too, with having created 'gentlemen' in *Dorian Gray* who left a room 'in a marked manner'. 'Have you ever seen it done?' he asked, superciliously. Later, of course, he would see just such a snub delivered to himself and his friend, and react with arrogant rage.

The greatest danger of friendship with Bosie was that he was an unstable member of an unstable family. Had he not been in love, Oscar's intelligence would have shown him that the affairs of the Douglases were too neurotically complicated for any outsider to take sides with safety. But he accepted Bosie's view entirely. According to Bosie, his father was a cruel and brutal man, who had treated his mother dreadfully badly. The Marquess had, indeed, introduced his mistress into his home, and proposed a *ménage à trois;* a proposal which led to his separation and ultimate divorce from his wife.

But Bosie was unable to recognise that his father had suffered too. As a bluff, unintellectual sportsman, with an old-fashioned love of the cruder pleasures in life, he would have cut an acceptable figure in the Regency aristocracy. He was not without independence and courage: he had noisily declared his atheism in public, and as a result had sacrificed Court favour and his right to sit as one of the representative Scottish peers in the House of Lords. What he wanted of his sons was to see them grow up as manly men, on his own sporting lines. Instead,

John Gray January 1893.

he had watched their mother develop their sensitivity, win their affection, and turn them against him. Bosie, the infant darling, was the extreme representative of this pattern. It was bad that he should be idling at Oxford to such an extent that he was often in danger of being sent down: worse that he should devote his leisure time to aesthetic poetry instead of hunting and whoring: and ultimately appalling that he should be consistently flippant and unanswerably insolent to his father, on whom he entirely depended for an allowance to support his extravagances. Queensberry was as much sinned against as sinning, but Oscar Wilde was unable to perceive this. And Wilde, as a leading aesthete, was from the first a suspect figure in the old Marquess's eyes.

From now on, Oscar and Bosie were to become inseparable. Writing plays for the commercial theatre involved making some attempt to meet deadlines, and generally having to work in ways that the indolent Oscar found rather tiresome. And so he made the need for peace and quiet an excuse to leave Constance overnight, and stay in hotels to work. Of course, Bosie spent much time in the hotels, distracting the work.

It was, however, in Tite Street, and not in a hotel, that Oscar actually seduced Bosie. They came back late at two in the morning after a performance of *Lady Windermere's Fan*. And their short-lived physical relationship began. Short-lived, because Bosie found Oscar unattractive. The older man was growing quite fat, and was becoming increasingly purple-faced and broken-veined. His prominent teeth, too, were in a bad state of decay, and he was self-conscious about this, putting a hand over his mouth when he laughed, so that he gave an unfortunate impression of coy tittering.

Nor can Bosie have been a particularly exciting or imaginative lover for Oscar. He permitted only such 'familiarities' as he had practised at Winchester, and resolutely eschewed what he called 'the sin which takes its name from one of the Cities of the Plain'. Really, both of them liked willing professional boys, and they were soon content to hunt them together, spending time with each other, flaunting their relationship in public, but not actually sleeping together. Their relationship was soon sufficiently proper for Bosie to stay with the Wildes, and, as he thought, win Constance's friendship.

At the end of 1892 the Wildes rented Lady Mount-Temple's house at Babbacombe Cliff, where Oscar wanted to write the play that would become *A Woman of No Importance*. Bosie stayed with them there, and when Constance went to visit friends in Florence, his tutor, Campbell Dodgson, also moved in with Oscar and the children. Some attempt was

made to persuade Bosie to do some work, and Oscar
described himself as the Headmaster of Babbacombe
School, for which he drew up a spoof list of rules:

Work. 11.30–12.30.
At 12.30
Sherry and biscuits for headmaster and boys
(the second master [i.e. Campbell Dodgson]
objects to this).
2.30–4.30.
Compulsory hide-and-seek for headmaster.
5.
Tea for headmaster and second master,
brandy and sodas (not to exceed seven) for boys.
12–1.30
Compulsory reading in bed. Any boy found
disobeying this rule will be immediately
woken up.

During his compulsory hide-and-seek Oscar
managed to complete *A Woman of No Importance*.
It was to be produced by Herbert Beerbohm Tree
at the Haymarket, although Oscar felt at first that
Tree was a totally unsuitable actor for his form of
melodramatic comedy. Tree was a master of
make-up, and revelled in creating stagey, larger-
than-life personalities. Yet he also had the gift for
realistic comedy: he was to create the role of
Professor Higgins in Shaw's *Pygmalion*, and proved
perfectly satisfactory as Wilde's Lord Illingworth.

Dissatisfaction did emerge during the rehearsals
but its cause was Oscar. Plays at this period did not
have clearly-defined producers or directors. Either
the author or an actor-manager might take on the
functions of a producer. Shaw, for example,
produced his own plays, with great success. Oscar
was full of ideas at rehearsals, but they did not
always seem sensible to the company. Nor did his
supercilious attitude to actors make him a popular
figure in the rehearsal rooms. Tree realised that he
was hindering the play's progress, and although a
man of as much sweetness of character as Oscar
himself, he reluctantly ordered that Mr Wilde was
not to be admitted to the theatre during rehearsals.
A few days before the opening, Tree was greatly
embarrassed to meet Oscar, strolling past the
Haymarket, and evidently hoping that his exclusion
might be rescinded. Tree could not cut him in the
street: he swept off his new top hat, hoping that the
gesture might obviate conversation. But Oscar,
determined to delay him, commented on the hat's
beautiful red silk lining. Spotting an exit line, Tree
ripped it out, and handed it to the astonished Oscar,
saying, 'Take it! It's yours!', before darting into
the theatre.

Working with Tree strengthened Oscar's ties with
the actor's twenty-three-years younger half-brother,
Max Beerbohm, who was enjoying a triumphant

right The playbill for the first production of
Lady Windermere's Fan.

right below A scene from the production.
Extreme left is Ben Webster as Cecil Graham,
and extreme right George Alexander as
Windermere.

below Bernard Partridge's reminder that
Oscar would face military conscription in
France if he carried out his threat to renounce
British citizenship.

bottom Sarah Bernhardt came to London in
1892 for the rehearsals of *Salome*. She
decided to use the costumes from her Paris
production of *Cléopâtre*, and the amount of
baggage she brought was noted by the press.

ST. JAMES'S THEATRE,

Sole Lessee and Manager - - Mr. GEORGE ALEXANDER.

On Saturday, February 20th, 1892, at 8 30 punctually, and Every Evening,
A New and Original Play, in Four Acts, by OSCAR WILDE, entitled

Lady Windermere's Fan

Lord Windermere	Mr. GEORGE ALEXANDER
Lord Darlington	Mr. NUTCOMBE GOULD
Lord Augustus Lorton	Mr. H. H. VINCENT
Mr. Charles Dumby	Mr. A. VANE TEMPEST
Mr. Cecil Graham	Mr. BEN WEBSTER
Mr. Hopper	Mr. ALFRED HOLLES
Parker	Mr. V. SANSBURY
Lady Windermere	Miss LILY HANBURY
The Duchess of Berwick	Miss FANNY COLEMAN
Lady Plimdale	Miss GRANVILLE
Mrs. Cowper-Cowper	Miss A. DE WINTON
Lady Jedburgh	Miss B. PAGE
Lady Agatha Carlisle	Miss LAURA GRAVES
Rosalie	Miss W. DOLAN
Mrs. Erlynne	Miss MARION TERRY

ACTS I & IV.	Morning-Room at Lord Windermere's, Carlton House Terrace	(*H. P. Hall*)
ACT II.	Drawing-Room at Lord Windermere's	(*Walter Hann*)
ACT III.	Lord Darlington's Rooms.	(*W. Harford*)

The Incidental Music by WALTER SLAUGHTER. The Furniture and Draperies by Messrs. FRANK GILES & Co., Kensington.
The Dresses by Mesdames SAVAGE and PURDUE. The Wigs by Mr. C. H. FOX. The Etchings and Engravings in the
corridors and vestibule kindly lent by Mr. I. P. MENDOZA, King Street, St. James's.

PROGRAMME OF MUSIC.

OVERTURE	"Marco Spado"	*Auber*	WALTZ	"Papillons Bleus"	*Waldteufel*
NEW BALLAD	"Stali"	*Walter Slaughter*	OVERTURE	"Il Seraglio"	*Mozart*
OVERTURE	"Le Caid"	*Ambroise Thomas*		"Toreador and Andalouse"	*Rubenstein*
INTERMEZZO	"Cavalleria Rusticana"	*Mascagni*	MELODIE	"Chant du Voyageur"	*Paderewski*

Doors open at 8.   Commence at 8 30.   Carriages at 11.

The Attendants are strictly forbidden to accept gratuities, and are liable to instant dismissal should they do so. Visitors to
the Theatre are earnestly begged to assist the Management in carrying out a regulation framed for their comfort and convenience.

Photographs of the Artistes may be obtained from ALFRED ELLIS, 20, Upper Baker Street, N W.

NO FEES.   THE THEATRE IS LIGHTED BY ELECTRICITY   **NO FEES.**
The Floral Decorations by HARROD'S STORES.

PRICES – Private Boxes £1 1s. to £4 4s ; Stalls, 10s. 6d ; Dress Circle, 7s and 5s ; Upper Boxes Numbered and Reserved
(Bonnets allowed) 4s ; Pit, 2s ; Gallery, 1s.
Box Office open daily from 10 till 5 o'clock   Seats can be Booked by Letter, Telegram, or Telephone No. 3903

Stage Manager ... ... Mr. ROBERT V. SHONE.   Musical Director ... Mr. WALTER SLAUGHTER.
    Business Manager ... ... Mr. ALWYN LEWIS.

A WILDE "TAG" TO A TAME PLAY.

SCENE—*A Theatre with Audience and Company complete. The former "smart" and languidly enthusiastic, the last wearily looking forward to the final " Curtain." The last Act is all but over.*

Servant (*to* Countess). The Duchess of BATTERSEA is in the Hall. May she come up?

Countess. Certainly. Why did you not show her up at once?

Servant (*arranging his powdered hair in a glass*). Because in cases of exposure her Grace is quite equal to showing up herself!

Countess (*smiling*). You are cynical, JOHN. Do you not know that cynicism is the birthright of fools, and, when discovered, is more than half found out?

Servant (*taking up coalscuttle*). Like the hair of your Ladyship—out of curl! [*Exit.*

Countess. A quaint conceit; but here is my husband. Let me avoid him. A married man is quite out of date—save when he forms the subject of his own obituary. [*Exit.*

A pause. Enter the Duchess *of* BATTERSEA.

Duchess. Dear me! No one here! So I might have brought the Duke with me, after all! And yet he is so fond of the petticoats. He loses his head when he begins kissing his hand. And I lose my head when I fail to catch a 'buss. A kiss with him and a 'buss with me—where's the difference?

Enter Earl PENNYPLAINE.

Earl (*angrily*). You here!

Duchess (*with an appealing gesture*). You are not pleased to see me! You regard me as an adventuress! You are ashamed of my past! A past unblessed by a clergyman—in fact, a past without a pastor!

Earl. Begone! Do not dare to darken my doors again. This is no home for old jokes!

Duchess. You must hear me. Do you know why I have treated you so badly? Do you know why I have taught your wife to regard me as a rival? Why I have blackmailed you to the tune of hundreds of thousands of pounds? Do you know why I have done all this and more? I will tell you. Because I am your Mother-in-law!

Earl (*in a choking voice*). I suspected as much from the very first!

Re-enter the Countess, *carrying a heap of family portraits.*

Countess. Here, Duchess, although you are not to my liking, I have brought you a few pictures of my husband and some of his predecessors. Take 'em, and bless you!

Duchess (*overflowing with emotion*). My dear, this is too much. (*Weeps.*) You unwoman—I should say unlady—me!

Enter Lord TUPPENCE CULLARD.

Lord T. C. Come and marry me.

Duchess. With pleasure! Lawks-a-mussy! [*Exeunt.*

Earl. And now, let us remember that while the sun shines, the moon clings like a frightened thing to the face of CLEOPATRA.

Quick Curtain.

Applause follows, when enter the Author. He holds between his thumb and forefinger a lighted cigarette.

Author. Ladies and Gentlemen, it is so much the fashion nowadays to do what one pleases, that I venture to offer you some tobacco while I enjoy a smoke myself. (*Throws cigars and cigarettes amongst the audience à la* HARRY PAYNE.) Will you forgive me if I change my tail-coat for a smoking jacket? Thank you! (*Makes the*

FANCY PORTRAIT.

QUITE TOO-TOO PUFFICKLY PRECIOUS!!
Being Lady Windy-mère's Fan-cy Portrait of the new dramatic author, Shakspeare Sheridan Oscar Puff, Esq.

["He addressed from the stage a public audience, mostly composed of ladies, pressing between his daintily-gloved fingers a still burning and half-smoked cigarette."—*Daily Telegraph.*]

necessary alteration of costume in the presence of the audience.) And now I will have a chair. (*Stamps, when up comes through a trap a table supporting a lounge*), and a cup of tea. (*Another table appears through another trap, bringing up with it a tray and a five o'clock set.*) And now I think we are comfortable. (*Helps himself to tea, smokes, &c.*) I must tell you I think my piece excellent. And all the puppets that have performed in it have played extremely well. I hope you like my piece as well as I do myself. I trust you are not bored with this chatter, but I am not good at a speech. However, as I have to catch a train in twenty minutes, I will tell you a story occupying a quarter of an hour. I repeat, as I have to catch a train—I repeat, as I have to catch a train——

Entire Audience. And so have we! [*Exeunt.* (*Thus the Play ends in smoke.*)

Punch reacts to Oscar's bad behaviour during his curtain speech.

right above John Sholto Douglas, the eighth Marquess of Queensberry.

right Lord Alfred Douglas with his elder brother Francis, Lord Drumlanrig.

undergraduate career at Oxford. Max was supremely elegant, splendidly witty, and a great admirer of Oscar. He introduced a fellow Mertonian, Reggie Turner, the illegitimate son of Lionel Lawson, part-owner of the *Daily Telegraph*, into Ross and Oscar's circle. Max, a romantic heterosexual, hoped that Ross would not lure Reggie into homosexual ways. He did not himself dislike Bosie Douglas but never became very close to him, partly because, as he shrewdly noted, 'he is obviously mad (like all his family I believe)'.

A Woman of No Importance was another triumph. On the second night the Prince of Wales came, commandeering the royal box from Mrs Langtry, and refusing to share it with his former friend. Oscar carefully refrained from repeating the offences of his first curtain speech. He quietly took his bow when called for, and did not even wear a green carnation, only a large bunch of lilies-of-the-valley.

Five months later, on the last night of the play's run, he was less circumspect. He went with Bosie, Ross (who was now known to his intimates as Robbie), and Aubrey Beardsley. All but Beardsley were very drunk, and Oscar was peculiarly affected and fatuous in his compliments to the actors. For the first time, Max Beerbohm felt quite repelled by him.

Aubrey Beardsley, always a sober member of Oscar's party, was not an intimate friend but, at this time, an artistic associate. The little consumptive insurance clerk had but recently been discovered. His wonderful mastery of sheer black mass and fine line on pure white had been exhibited for the first time in 1892. He was evidently a major talent, and John Lane, who published decadent writers without ever very much liking them personally, engaged him to illustrate an English version of *Salome*. Bosie undertook the translation while on holiday with Oscar at Goring, though Oscar did not approve of the final version, and made some alterations. Beardsley's illustrations did not win the approval of either author or publisher. Oscar had two grounds for disliking them. The first was sheerly artistic, and quite reasonable. Aubrey's drawings, he complained, were Japanese, whereas his play was Byzantine. Put into simple English this meant that Beardsley's art was technically clean, precise, and direct, whereas Wilde's was lush, ornate and heavy. Both were artificial and decadent, but in quite different ways. Oscar's second objection was harder to confess. Beardsley had wickedly caricatured him in some of his drawings of Herod, using the now bloated Aesthete's sensual features to express the character's corrupt lasciviousness.

Lane's objection was much simpler. He thought that some of the pictures were indecent, and demanded that several be re-drawn. It was Lane who

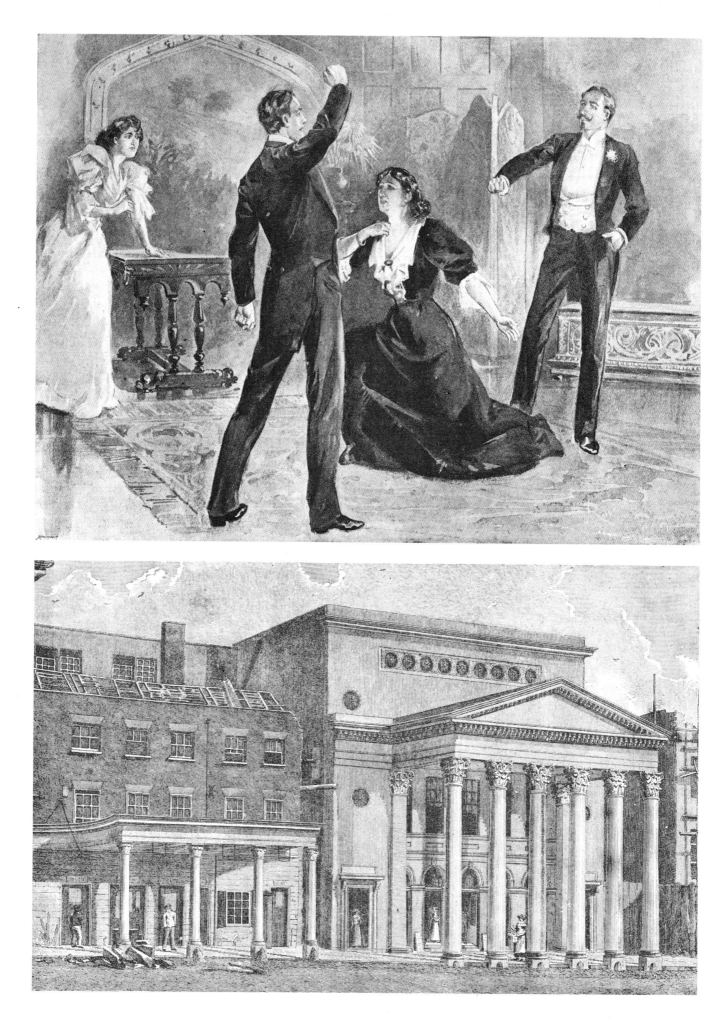

produced the revoltingly mealy-mouthed and anatomically inaccurate title 'The Stomach Dance' for one of Beardsley's best-known illustrations.

But it might have been better for Oscar had he too raised public objections to the supposed indecency of Beardsley's work. The young man had an astounding talent for suggesting, in an economically drawn smirk or leer, that a whole personality was consumed with itching lust. Wilde's play, of course, did no such thing. His Herod was indeed lubricious. His Herodias was simply an exotically jealous wife, fearful that her daughter was the object of her husband's desire. Salome's private passion for Jokanaan played along that strange psychological knife-edge where religious and sexual yearnings meet and intertwine.

But Beardsley's characters looked *knowing*. They were not in the grip of poetic passions: it was obvious that they *did* things, and a part of them wanted to laugh at the respectable Victorian public that didn't. Lane's insistence on the decorous excision of breasts, navels, and penises did nothing to conceal the fact that Beardsley's drawings appealed to a feeling that sex was evil, and very, very desirable. The literary content of Beardsley's beautiful decorations was, literally, meretricious. And so, with the publication of *Salome* in 1894, Oscar Wilde was again unhappily associated in the Philistine mind with the publication of a salacious book, which he claimed was 'art'.

Reggie Turner, drawn by his fellow-Mertonian, Max Beerbohm.

left above A scene from the first production. Mrs Beere as Mrs Arbuthnot and Tree as Lord Illingworth.

left The Haymarket Theatre, where Tree presented *A Woman of No Importance* in 1893. On the left the earlier theatre is shown being demolished.

Actually, co-operation with Wilde proved more difficult than Lane or Beardsley had bargained for. When Lane proposed a new quarterly journal of creative work in an expensive format, with Beardsley as its art editor, both agreed that Wilde should have nothing to do with it. And so it transpired that the best-known publication of the nineties, *The Yellow Book*, appeared without any contribution from the best-known man of letters of the time. He was obviously piqued by the omission. He told Bosie that the first number was 'dull and loathesome, a great failure', and added, 'I am so glad.'

In the end Beardsley's caution was of no avail. He himself continued to be too daring for Lane, and kept having to re-draw covers. Soon, on the urging of William Watson, an even more dully conservative poet than Henley, Beardsley was dismissed. And with his wit, audacity and elegance removed, the raft of distinguished contributors were unable to give life to the quarterly numbers.

1894 was a notably yellow year. In addition to the publication of *Salome* and *The Yellow Book* it saw the appearance of *The Sphinx*, the long ornate poem on which Wilde had been working on and off since his first visit to Paris. Again Lane produced the book, although Wilde was becoming increasingly certain that the publisher did not care for his work.

Punch produced a skit on *The Sphinx*, but Oscar was no longer offended by *Punch's* squibs. For now they were written by a dear friend, Mrs Ada Leverson. He had met her in 1892, and instantly enjoyed her light wit and bright intelligence. She could understand and appreciate his work; she recognised his kindness and generosity; she was prosperous, fashionable and extravagant; she was utterly without the dullness and conventionality of Constance, who was by now taking a serious interest in spiritualism and shared Lady Mount-Temple's enthusiasm for Madame Blavatsky of the questionable reputation. Although Ada's sketches in *Punch* were not particularly funny, Oscar knew they were written without malice, and he had no objection to her calling his hifalutin sphinx 'The Minx'. He had long been fascinated by the mythical Egyptian monster. He had called women 'sphinxes without secrets' – one of his *mots* that sounded sharp, but meant little on examination. *The Sphinx Without a Secret* had been the flattest of the little collection of short stories he had issued with *Lord Arthur Savile's Crime* in 1891. And from now on he nicknamed Ada 'Sphinx'.

At first, Oscar and Bosie believed that the Sphinx was the author of *The Green Carnation*, a mildly satirical novel which appeared anonymously in 1894, and lampooned them as Esmè Amarinth and Lord Reginald Hastings. But they soon found out that the real author was an unknown young writer called

Aubrey Beardsley, self-portrait.

The art of Aubrey Beardsley, showing his mastery of black mass and fine line and the luxurious, decadent effect he achieved without using colour. This design for a title page for *Salome* *(left)* was far too daring for John Lane, the publisher, who suppressed it.

right 'The Entrance of Herodias'. The owl-capped jester is Oscar Wilde. This was suppressed by John Lane.

below 'The Eyes of Herod' and 'Salome with the head of John The Baptist': decadence and barbarism expressed with supreme elegance. Beardsley's favourite quasi-phallic candles and trellised roses are combined with the peacock and butterfly made fashionable by Whistler. Wilde objected to Beardsley's clean-lined 'Japanese' drawings; he wanted something lush and 'Byzantine'. He also objected to being portrayed as a lascivious Herod.

Robert Hichens who had met Bosie in Egypt, where
the despairing Lady Queensberry had made an
abortive effort to start her son on a diplomatic
career. They sent Hichens comic threatening
telegrams, though really they quite enjoyed the
notoriety the book brought. But any sort of gossip
about their relationship was only likely to do them
harm.

At the end of the summer they stayed together in
Worthing. Wilde was working on a new play for
George Alexander, and Douglas was either helping
or distracting him. Daily they went down to the
beach. Oscar was a surprisingly good swimmer, and
enjoyed his daily dip. But the beach was also the
haunt of boys: fishermen's boys, newspaper-vendors,
working-class lads who were happy to be taken up
by 'the Lord' and his rich friend. Although Oscar
was not at this time rich; only extravagant. The
earnings from his plays were spent in frenzied
luxury with Bosie. And, it must be added, wonderful
generosity to quite simple and deserving people.
From the profits of *Lady Windermere's Fan* Oscar
made a spontaneous gift of £160 to a young solicitor
whom he heard lamenting the fact that he could not
afford to get married. A young clerk of Lane's, who
had been seduced by Oscar, and then left him
suddenly, wrote in neurotic and guilt-ridden strains
begging for money. 'As he betrayed me grossly I, of
course, gave him money and was kind to him,' Oscar
told Bosie. And he was probably doing himself no
more than justice.

But his reputation was suffering all the time.
When he went to Florence to meet Bosie on his
return from Cairo, André Gide observed that he was
looking older and uglier than he had done in Paris.
In London, Frank Harris, who proved
astoundingly naive when confronted with a sexuality
that did not involve women, was puzzled to find
Oscar dining with uneducated grooms whose cockney
accents grated on the snobbish ears of 1890s literary
society. And in Pimlico, a very sinister friend
suffered an unwelcome visit from the police. Alfred
Taylor, a dissolute ex-public schoolman who had
squandered his fortune, ran a house of assignation
for transvestites and male prostitutes. His rooms
were raided at a time when Wilde was not there, but
too many shady people knew that he frequented the
place. And it was indiscreet of him to write a
sympathetic letter about the raid to Taylor's
partner.

Not that Oscar and Bosie had ever been discreet.
While *A Woman of No Importance* was running at
the Haymarket, a blackmailer tried to sell Beerbohm
Tree one of Oscar's letters to Bosie. He had acquired
it from a renter he employed to steal compromising
material. Tree informed Oscar, who was thus

far left Oscar and Bosie, 1894.

left A bazaar in Algiers, where Oscar, Bosie and André Gide enjoyed a scandalous holiday at the beginning of 1895.

below A caricature of Oscar by Max Beerbohm, 1894. Beerbohm was appalled to find, a year later, that his work was to be used by the police to reinforce Queensberry's allegations.

forewarned when the scoundrel turned up at Tite Street demanding money. With lofty scorn Oscar pretended to treat the matter as a sale of literary manuscripts, berated the man for having allowed so precious a document to become dirty, and suggested that an original Wilde autograph should fetch a great deal more money than he was asking. Cowed, the blackmailer sent a henchman to return the letter, saying it was no use renting Oscar as he only laughed at them. But the repurchase of compromising letters had already cost Wilde £10, and he took hasty steps to have Pierre Louÿs translate this particular document into French, so that it might be passed off as an exercise in poetic prose.

1895 was the year of catastrophe. Yet it opened as the most golden of golden years. In January Lewis Waller opened *An Ideal Husband* at the Haymarket, and at the end of the month Oscar went to Algiers to squander the receipts with Bosie. They met André Gide there, and enjoyed a month of unrestrained debauchery with Arab boys. Then in February Alexander opened *The Importance of Being Earnest* at the St James's, and Oscar enjoyed the triumph of having two of the most successful plays in London running concurrently.

Earnest is a farce of perfect charm, utterly removed from the sphere of real moral problems, which had been handled so melodramatically in Wilde's earlier comedies. To Shaw and Shaw alone has this ever seemed a weakness. Contemporaries recognised in Wilde a talent for comic dialogue unmatched since Congreve, but were unwilling to note that the absence of all cruelty makes *Earnest* a more delightful play than any Restoration comedy. Wilde had artistically learned the importance of not being earnest.

The first night was an unparalleled success. Our respectable grandparents simply yelled their enthusiasm. Allan Aynesworth, who played Algernon, saw nothing like it in the whole of his successful career. Oscar Wilde was on a pinnacle.

CATASTROPHE

'Not a year passes in England without somebody disappearing. Scandals used to lend charm, or at least interest, to a man – now they crush him.'

'The screaming Scarlet Marquis', as Oscar nicknamed Bosie's father, lunched in the Café Royal in 1892. Bosie called him over to the table where Oscar and he were sitting, and the suspicious red-whiskered sportsman suddenly found himself deluged in a sea of charm. At two o'clock Bosie had to leave, but Wilde and Queensberry stayed talking till four. The next day Bosie received a letter from his father assuring him that his friendship with Wilde was quite all right – 'He is a wonderful man.'

But rumours and gossip continued to reach the marquess. Plans for him to visit the Wildes on holiday came to nothing. Bosie grew increasingly insolent. In 1894 Queensberry lunched in the Café Royal again, and this time he was appalled to witness his son's flagrantly gay mannerisms.

'With my own eyes,' he wrote in a fury the next day, 'I saw you both in the most loathsome and disgusting relationship as expressed by your manner and expression. Never in my experience have I seen such a sight as that in your horrible features. No wonder people are talking as they are.' To this paternal tirade, Bosie replied with the languid telegram, 'What a funny little man you are.'

Now Queensberry was determined to humiliate Wilde publicly, and terminate the friendship with his son. Since Bosie was unamenable to threats, the marquess took a friend with him, and paid a call at Tite Street. Householder and visitor gave different accounts of the angry confrontation. According to Queensberry, Wilde 'showed the white feather'. But according to Wilde, he told the marquess that whatever the Queensberry rules might be, 'the Oscar Wilde rule is to shoot at sight', and with that put the furious father out of his house, first telling his manservant that the Marquess of Queensberry was 'the most infamous brute in London', and must never again be admitted.

Bosie was rather in favour of using firearms as a defence against his parent. He caused a ridiculous incident when he accidentally fired a pistol-shot into a ceiling at the Berkeley Hotel. But at this time the infatuated Oscar could see no blemish in his friend's conduct.

Wilde's theatrical triumphs were more than the marquess could stand. He had, in the past, created a disturbance in a theatre where a play of Tennyson's was reputed to ridicule atheists. Queensberry had thrown a bunch of root vegetables on to the stage, and then harangued the audience. Now he planned to disrupt *The Importance of Being Earnest* in the same way. A friend warned Wilde, and the theatre staff were able to intercept Queensberry and refuse him admittance. But the threat of harrassment seemed intolerable to Wilde.

He was at the peak of his fame. His plays were at last giving him means beyond which he could live with opulence. He could buy young men from Pimlico to Paris, from Italy to Algiers, and bask in their self-abasement before his money, as the gilded youth of London and Oxford bowed to his wit and charm. In the enchanted cloud of adulation there was but one hostile threat: Queensberry. To Oscar Wilde, all his success and happiness seemed no more than his natural deserts. Any challenge to his supremacy seemed an unnatural evil. He would brook no unforgiving enemy, for he had ceased to believe that he need extend tolerance beyond the point at which his innate kindness made it a pleasure. In the pictures of him in these years, the camera shows a face of almost weak gentleness, but the painter shows the same features wearing a mask of overweening arrogance. And both show the truth.

Refused his uproar at the theatre, the Marquess of Queensberry made his way to the Albemarle Club, where he left his card, endorsed 'To Oscar Wilde posing as a somdomite' – a mis-spelling which was to become famous. The porter, with wise discretion, put the card in an envelope, and ten days later handed it to Wilde when he visited the club. As he handed it over, he calmly assured the recipient that he had not understood what it meant.

right The year 1895 saw the peak of Oscar Wilde's worldly success. *An Ideal Husband* opened on 3 January at the Haymarket Theatre, and was such a success that the run was extended. The play closed when the playwright was disgraced.

below Scenes from *An Ideal Husband.* Charles Hawtrey (p. 107) and Charles Brookfield (not seen here), though they enjoyed the benefits of the play's long run, seem to have nursed a spiteful hatred for Oscar: they gave a dinner for Queensberry after the trial, and a rumour persisted for years that they had actually gathered evidence for him.

Theatre Royal Haymarket.

Sole Lessee	... ... Mr. TREE.
Managers	... Mr. LEWIS WALLER AND Mr. H. H. MORELL.

Mr. TREE begs to announce that during his absence in America his Theatre has been taken for the Spring Season by Mr. LEWIS WALLER and Mr. H. H. MORELL.

On THURSDAY, JANUARY 3rd, at 8 o'clock.

A New and Original Play of Modern Life, entitled

AN IDEAL HUSBAND,

By OSCAR WILDE.

The Earl of Caversham, K.G.	Mr. ALFRED BISHOP
Lord Goring ... (his Son) ...	Mr. CHARLES H. HAWTREY
Sir Robert Chiltern	Mr. LEWIS WALLER
(Under Secretary for Foreign Affairs)	
Vicomte de Nanjac	Mr. COSMO STUART
Mr. Montford	Mr. HENRY STANFORD
Phipps	Mr. C. H. BROOKFIELD
Mason	Mr. H. DEANE
Footman ... ... (at Lord Goring's) ...	Mr. CHARLES MEYRICK
Footman ... (at Sir Robert Chiltern's) ...	Mr. GOODHART
Lady Chiltern	Miss JULIA NEILSON
Lady Markby	Miss FANNY BROUGH
Lady Basildon	Miss VANE FEATHERSTON
Mrs. Marchmont	Miss HELEN FORSYTH
Miss Mabel Chiltern ... (Sir Robert's Sister)	Miss MAUDE MILLETT
Mrs. Cheveley	Miss FLORENCE WEST

But Wilde lost his head completely. He immediately looked to Robbie and Bosie for sympathy: he had received a card 'with hideous words on it': 'the tower of ivory was assailed by the foul thing'.

The instant Ross received Wilde's hysterical note, he rushed round to the Avondale Hotel and began to give bad advice. Alfred Douglas, seeing a chance to have his hated father imprisoned for criminal libel, was all for Wilde's taking legal action. But as Douglas knew, George Lewis was the most competent solicitor for Wilde to instruct. Unhappily, Wilde seems to have felt that he had bothered Lewis too often with homosexual problems, and feared that it was damaging his social relations with the *haut monde's* solicitor. Instead, he accepted Ross's recommendation of his own solicitor, Charles Humphreys. And so, on 1 March 1895, advised by a lawyer who knew nothing of his life and accepted his statement that there was no truth in the suggestion that he 'posed as a sodomite', Oscar Wilde applied for a warrant against the Marquess of Queensberry. A day later Bosie had the satisfaction of seeing his father arrested and brought before the Marlborough Street magistrates.

At the preliminary hearings it became clear that Queensberry had no evidence to put forward but some of the indiscreet letters Oscar had written to Bosie, and innuendoes against his published works. Elated with the prospect of success, Oscar and Bosie went to Monte Carlo where they squandered money they had borrowed for their legal expenses. A palmist in whom they reposed complete confidence had promised them victory, and it was only during the long hours that Bosie spent at the gaming tables that Oscar wondered whether he had taken a dangerous course.

Queensberry wasted no time in such idle follies. He instructed Lewis to act for him, and Lewis briefed Edward Carson to appear in court. The barrister, like the solicitor, had expected to be asked to act for the fashionable plaintiff and either would, in that case, probably have prevented the disastrous dénouement. But Humphreys had briefed the upright Sir Edward Clarke, who knew nothing about the homosexual underworld, and accepted that he was appearing for an innocent man who had been most horribly and scandalously libelled.

While Oscar and Bosie quarrelled and gambled in Monaco, the defence engaged private detectives to investigate the extent of the 'sodomitical pose'. A disgruntled prostitute, who naively believed that rich homosexuals attracted clients away from her trade, gave a lead to Alfred Taylor's establishment, and suddenly Queensberry had his hands on a nest of renters and blackmailers who could be threatened and cajoled into giving evidence of Wilde's secret

below George Alexander, actor-manager and lessee of the St James's Theatre from 1891 until his death in 1918. He produced *The Importance of being Earnest* on 14 February and both playwright and star enjoyed a triumph. Like most of fashionable London he behaved badly after the trial: he removed the author's name from the playbills, and took advantage of Wilde's bankruptcy to secure the rights in *Earnest* and *Lady Windermere*. He made some amends later, with voluntary payments to Wilde, and he bequeathed the rights to Oscar's sons when he died.

below right Charles Hawtrey.

life. Oscar came back to London to find his counsel studying a proof of evidence from the defence which now went far beyond the suggestion that a famous writer assumed a distastefully camp manner in his private letters and public writings. If Clarke had known anything about the world from which Queensberry was drawing his new witnesses he would surely have advised Wilde to drop the case. But he accepted, instead, his client's airy assurance that these were mere perjurers, somehow bought by Queensberry from squalid areas of society with which innocent Oscar had no real acquaintance.

Other friends gave Oscar good advice. Bernard Shaw had begun writing plays at about the same time as his compatriot, and Oscar had generously treated him as the other member of a 'great Celtic school', although Shaw's first plays enjoyed no success, while Wilde's were a triumph. Their friendly relations had cooled slightly, possibly through Shaw's inability to disguise his inevitable contempt for Willie Wilde, but there had been no outright quarrel. Shaw and Frank Harris now met Wilde in the Café Royal. He wanted them to give expert evidence as to the moral worth of *Dorian Gray*. Both were willing to do so but both urged that he drop the case, not because either suggested that he was a practising pederast, but because it was apparent to them that a Victorian jury would take the view that Queensberry, rightly or wrongly, was trying to protect his son, and therefore would have to be forgiven and acquitted of any libel he might inadvertently have committed under the stress of moral paternal feeling. Bosie came in to hear this advice, and furiously prevented Oscar from yielding to it. He marched his champion out of the restaurant, roundly telling the two writers that they were no friends to give Oscar such advice. Even Oscar weakly murmured that it 'really was not friendly of you, Frank'.

Alfred Douglas's optimistic energy rested on an aspect of his personality as yet untested. He was to prove one of the most litigious men of his generation, and obsessively longed to address the world from the witness-box. In 1895 he was quite sure that he could win the case by giving evidence against his father and proving that he had never been a responsible parent. Clarke, of course, would not hear of any such irrelevant evidence. Alfred and his brother Percy had to content themselves with offering to finance the plaintiff's case (until, as they assumed, he should win back costs from their father). Alfred put up £300; Percy promised the balance, and Oscar borrowed £500 from Ada Leverson's husband Ernest.

The trial of the Marquess of Queensberry opened at the Old Bailey on 3 April 1895. The plaintiff was almost his own sole witness, and the greater part of the proceedings was taken up with his cross-examination by Carson.

Wilde opened badly. Like Speranza, he was habitually above some truths; among them, his age. Carson was able to reduce him to fumbling with his opening questions by demonstrating that Wilde had not only presented himself to the court as being two years younger than he actually was, but seemed unwilling ever to be frank about this quite unimportant matter.

But as the cross-examination turned to the literary reputation of Oscar Wilde, the witness recovered his aplomb. He had, after all, never written anything with a deliberately pornographic or aphrodisiac intent, and he knew that he was justified in contemptuously rejecting the suggestion that his books were corruptly tinged with homosexuality. As he recovered confidence, he recovered wit, and began to delight his friends in the public gallery with the smart answers he returned.

Carson tried, with barrister's literalism, to analyse

what was going on in *Dorian Gray*, and Wilde skipped deftly through impudence to dumb insolence:

Q. Let us go over it phrase by phrase. 'I quite admit that I adored you madly.' What do you say to that? Have you ever adored a young man madly?

A. No; not madly. I prefer love; that is a higher form.

Q. Never mind about that. Let us keep down to the level we are at now.

A. I have never given adoration to anybody except myself.

Q. I suppose you think that a very smart thing?

A. Not at all.

Wilde the playwright could see when Carson's elaborate questions cued him for flat denials:

Q. I believe you have written an article to show that Shakespeare's sonnets were suggestive of unnatural vice.

A. On the contrary, I have written an article to show that they are not.

And he stung his questioner to irritation when he slipped words around him as though he were himself the smooth, be-wigged cross-examiner, thoroughly at home with confusing witnesses:

Q. (reading) 'I adored you extravagantly' –

A. Do you mean financially?

Q. Oh, yes, financially! Do you think we are talking about finance?

A. I do not know what you are talking about.

As long as literature was in question Carson could not begin to break through Wilde's guard. The plaintiff complacently established that he regarded the Oxford undergraduate magazine to which he had submitted some recent aphorisms as 'worse than immoral – it was badly written'. And by cool effrontery he was able to slip away from the damaging implications of the indiscreet letters he had sent Bosie. He was extremely lucky that Carson omitted a sentence in which he had said he would sooner be rented by every blackmailer in London than put up with Bosie's scenes: either the camp jargon was incomprehensible to the lawyers, or else Carson took a generous and unprofessional risk at his own client's expense, and refrained from producing the really damning condemnation of Wilde out of his own mouth. But he hammered away at the precious over-writing which filled the letters: 'You are the divine thing I want, the thing of grace and beauty...'; 'it is a marvel that those red rose-leaf lips of yours should have been made no less for the music of song than for madness of kisses'; 'Your slim gilt soul walks between passion and poetry.'

'Is that a beautiful phrase?' Carson asked rhetorically of this last, and had his sarcasm put down

Sir Edward Clarke, Wilde's counsel in all three cases. A man so punctilious that he preferred not to accept briefs unless sure that justice lay on his client's side, he nonetheless continued to appear for Wilde after he knew that his client was not only guilty, but had misled him personally. Cartoon by Spy.

right London in the 1890s. Oxford Circus and, below, Piccadilly Circus with newly erected (1893) Shaftesbury memorial fountain. Popularly known as 'Eros', Alfred Gilbert's sculpture is itself a striking example of Art Nouveau introduced as the centrepiece of a great public place.

with, 'Not as you read it, Mr Carson. You read it very badly.'

It was during the second day of cross-examination that Carson began to come out on top. He stopped trying to infer sodomy from a decadent prose style, and moved on to the much stronger ground of Wilde's working-class juvenile associates. Did Wilde know Alfred Taylor? And Charles Parker? And his brother William? A valet and a groom? And Ernest Scarfe, another valet? And Charles Hickey? And Edward Shelley? Charles Mason? Alphonse Conway? Only the previous evening Wilde had told a friend he had nothing to worry about – 'The working classes are with me – to a boy!' Now his 'feasting with panthers' was being exposed to a wider public, and he could muster little defence for it.

It may, to some extent, have been true, as Wilde claimed, that he always enjoyed the company of those who for one reason or another lived outside the bounds of respectable society, and admired their love of freedom. Sherard, for example, remembered his talking for hours with an unsavoury petty criminal and Paris police informer called Bibi-le-Purée. But it was hopeless to claim credit for this democratic spirit in a cross-examination which he had opened by declaring himself the most élitist of artists. When he was asked why he spent time with a newspaper boy, it was witty to say that it was the first time he had heard of the boy's being connected with literature. But it could only remind the court that he had made very high-handed claims for his own literary seriousness in justifying his letters to Douglas. It was wise to reply 'Certainly not', when asked if he had ever kissed a certain boy, but it was utter folly to add the camp frivolity, 'He was a very ugly boy,' in explanation. Carson quickly reduced him to fumbling embarrassment after that answer.

When Oscar Wilde left the witness-box it was clear that he had lost his case. When Carson's opening speech for the defence stated that the boys named were going to appear and testify, Clarke told his client that the case must be abandoned before they could do so, and advised him to leave the country in any case, before criminal proceedings were started against him.

Now came Wilde's terrible loss of nerve, and the vile furore of national moralising, as the great scandal swept to its tragic conclusion. He had a day in which to leave the country, and the authorities seemed at first less vindictive than the public and press. The unquestionably wicked attempt to have Queensberry gaoled for an offence he had not committed had failed. Oscar Wilde could have preserved himself by quick and discreet flight to France. Instead he sat in the Cadogan Hotel with Ross and the Douglas brothers, drinking hock-and-seltzer, and wondering what had gone wrong. He resisted their encouragement to flight with feeble excuses. The police, meanwhile, decently waited to give him time to catch the boat-train. When it had left, and they finally came to the hotel, Wilde was quietly drunk, and hazily interested in the process of being arrested. He took Pierre Louÿs's *Aphrodite* with him to read in the cells, and its yellow cover led to the rumour that he was reading *The Yellow Book* at the time of his arrest. Public indignation helped sink Lane's quarterly cultural venture in the great débâcle of the nineties.

A few people behaved well. Carson refused to accept the crown's brief against Wilde. He had done his duty for his client, and bore no malice toward the witness who had scored off him. Clarke continued to act for a client who had lied to him, and so caused

left Edward Carson, Wilde's student contemporary at Trinity College, Dublin, appeared for Queensberry in the libel case. After suffering some contemptuous flicks of Wilde's wit, Carson proceeded to crush him in cross-examination. Subsequently he urged colleagues to withdraw from further prosecution of Wilde. From a portrait by John Lavery.

below John Gielgud as John Worthing and Edith Evans as Lady Bracknell, parts which they made very much their own, in a 1939 production of *The Importance of being Earnest* at the Globe Theatre, London. Gwendolen was played by Joyce Carey, Algy by Ronald Ward.

WILDE LIBEL ACTION.

MARQUIS OF QUEENSBERRY ON TRIAL.

EVIDENCE OF PROSECUTOR.

STRANGE LETTERS.

SENSATIONAL TERMINATION.

WILDE ARRESTED.

All the appearances of a sensational trial were presented at the Old Bailey on Wednesday, when the Marquis of Queensberry entered the dock to answer the charge of criminally libelling Mr. Oscar Wilde. The marquis was the first to appear, and was soon followed by Mr. Oscar Wilde, who took a seat at the solicitors' table. By the time Mr Justice Collins took his seat on the bench the court was crammed. Sir E. Clarke, Mr. Mathews, and Mr. Humphreys appeared to prosecute, while Mr. Carson, Mr. Gill, and Mr. A. Gill represented the Marquis of Queensberry. Mr. Besley, with Mr. Monckton, watching the proceedings on behalf of Lord Douglas of Hawick, eldest son of the marquis.—The clerk read out the indictment to the effect that the marquis "did unlawfully and maliciously write and publish a false, malicious, and defamatory libel" concerning Mr. O. Wilde, in the form of a card directed to him.—The marquis said he pleaded not guilty, and that the libel was true, and that it was for the public benefit that it should be published.—Sir E. Clarke having opened the case for the prosecution, evidence was given by Sydney Wright, hall porter of the Albemarle Club, of the publication of the alleged libel.—Mr. Oscar Wilde was then called and examined. After giving evidence as to his University and literary career, he said: In 1884 I married Miss Lloyd, and from that time up to now I have lived with her in Chelsea and other places. I have two sons. In 1891 I made the acquaintance of Lord A. Douglas. He was brought by a friend of mine to my house in Chelsea. Since 1891 I have been acquainted with Lady Queensberry, and have been a guest at her house many times. I have also been on friendly terms with Lord A. Douglas's brother, Lord Douglas of Hawick. Lord A. Douglas has stayed at my house on numerous occasions. In November, 1894, I was lunching with Lord A. Douglas in the public room at the Café Royal. I was aware that there was some estrangement between Lord A. Douglas and Lord Queensberry. The latter entered the room, and, at my suggestion, Lord Alfred crossed the room and shook hands with his father. Lord Alfred had to go away early, and Lord Queensberry remained and chatted with me. Afterwards something was said about Torquay, and it was arranged that Lord Queensberry should call upon me there, but he did not come. It was in 1893 that I heard that some letters which I had written to Lord A. Douglas had come into possession of certain persons. I met a man named Wood, who said he had some letters which had been written by me, which he had found in a suit of clothes that Lord A. Douglas had given him. I said, "You certainly should have given them back to him." He took three or four letters from his pocket and said, "Here are the letters." I read them and remarked, "I do not consider these letters of any importance," and the man replied, "They were stolen from me the day before yesterday by a man named Allen. I have only just got them back again, as they wished to extort money from you." I observed, "I do not consider that they are of any value at all." He said, "I am very much afraid of staying in London, as these men are threatening me; I want to go to America." I asked him what hope of success he had in America better than London, and he replied that he must get out of London. He made a very strong appeal to me to enable him to go to New York, as he could find nothing to do in London. I gave him £16.—Witness was next cross-examined as to the man Wood, and he said he was a

MARQUIS OF QUEENSBERRY.

OSCAR WILDE.

YOUNG MAN OF NO OCCUPATION.

They dined together at the Florence Restaurant. He was asked to be kind to him by Lord Alfred Douglas. He did not care for a man's social position. Wood was not an artist. He gave Wood £16.—Mr. Carson: I suggest that the next day you gave him another £5. That is so. I gave it to him as he represented that he should otherwise arrive in America without a penny.—Mr. Carson: Do you really suggest that you gave him the £21 out of charity? It is not for me to might look more like your equal?—Witness: Oh, no; he could not look like that. (Laughter.)—The witness was under examination when the case was adjourned.—The case was continued on Thursday.—Resuming his cross-examination by Mr. Carson, prosecutor said it was Taylor who brought about his introduction to Wood. He had frequently been to Taylor's house for afternoon tea parties, at 13, Little College-street. Witness did not think Taylor kept any servants. The furniture did not appear luxurious, but was in good taste. He had certainly been to see him when the gas and candles were not lit. It would not be true to say that the gas and candles were always alight. He believed that once, in the month of March, he saw him about 12, when there was no light. Taylor was in the habit of burning perfumes in the room. He knew that Taylor and Parker were afterwards arrested by the police. He knew Parker well, and had invited him to his house. Parker's brother came and had dinner with him the first time they met. When he met Parker it was at a dinner. Parker's brother was with him. He did not know that the brothers were then respectively a valet and a groom out of employment. He did not take the one he called "Charlie" with him to the Savoy Hotel that night, nor did he give him any money. He

FIRST GAVE HIM MONEY

on Dec. 1, 1893. That was at a private dinner. Between October, 1893, and February, 1894, he had rooms at St. James's-street, though he still lived in Tite-street. He remembered Parker coming there to tea on four or five occasions. Sometimes Parker would be alone, and sometimes with Taylor. He had given him money to the extent of £3, but no impropriety had taken place. He had never visited Park Walk at 12 o'clock at night to see Parker. He had not seen him since February, 1893, but he believed he had enlisted in the Army. When Parker and Taylor were arrested they were in women's clothes, and were charged with felonious practices.—Mr. Carson: When you read of Taylor's arrest did it make any difference in your friendship towards him.—Witness: I was greatly distressed, and wrote to him, but it had made no difference. The man Fred Atkins was in the employ of a bookmaker. Witness first met Atkins at the rooms of the gentleman whose name had been handed to the judge. He met him at a dinner where Taylor was present. He felt friendly towards him, and called him by his Christian name. They went to Paris and stayed together, he (witness) paying the fare. This, however, was subsequently repaid him, but not by Atkins. No impropriety took place while there, and it would be an infamous lie for anyone to say so. They stayed together in Paris until Saturday. Continuing, witness said he had simply taken Atkins to Paris to please his friend, and not disappoint the lad. After he came back he was very ill, and confined to his bed, and Atkins and the gentleman who had introduced them came to see him in his room. He would swear that Atkins was not in the room alone.

HE GAVE ATKINS £3 15s.

and some presents, and took tea with him twice in his rooms. That was to hear him sing, as he said he wished to go on the music hall stage. Witness knew a young man named Scarfe, but denied all impropriety. A young man named Maher had stayed with him at a hotel, though he lived in London at the time. He was very nice and charming, and he gave him a cigarette case value £4. He knew Walter Grainger, who was servant to Lord Alfred Douglas.—Mr. Carson: Did you ever kiss the boy?—Witness: No, never; certainly not. He was an extremely ugly boy.—Mr. Carson: Was that the reason why you did not kiss him?—Witness: Oh, Mr. Carson, you are pertinently insolent.—Mr. Carson: Why, sir, did you mention that this boy was extremely ugly?—Witness: I do not know why I mentioned that he was ugly except that I was stung by the insolent questions you put to me, and the way

YOU HAVE INSULTED ME

throughout this hearing. He absolutely denied that one of the masseurs at the Savoy Hotel had ever seen him in a compromising situation, or that any misconduct had ever taken place with a man named Scarfe. Mr. Wilde first met Scarfe, he said, in December, 1893; was introduced to him by Taylor; he was about 20, and of no occupation at that time, but had been out in the Australian gold diggings. Taylor brought him round simply because Scarfe had interested Lord Hawick on board ship on the way to Australia, and it was simply for the same reason that Mr. Wilde gave him "one of Kettner's best, with the best of Kettner's wine." He had never kissed or caressed the youth. He had given him a silver cigarette case; but that, said Mr. Wilde, was "because I am so good-natured, and because it is a custom of mine to give cigarette cases."—Mr. Carson held up a silver case.—"No, really," burst out the author, "I could not. I have given so many I could not recognise one from another." Keeping the rooms which Lord Hawick and Lord Alfred Douglas occupied at Oxford was a lad of 16, named Walter Grainger. Questions regarding him were also asked, and Mr. Wilde caused some laughter by saying he was ugly. Shortly afterwards the startling cross-examination came to a close. Mr. Carson sat down, Mr. Wilde drew a breath of relief, and Sir Edward Clarke rose to ask his client a few questions. Sir E. Clarke produced a batch of correspondence which had passed between

LORD QUEENSBERRY AND HIS SON,

Lord A. Douglas. The first letter by the marquis was painful and pathetic in a high degree. It began with a complaint of the tone of the letters previously received from Lord known by all some day that Rosebery not only insulted me by

LYING TO THE QUEEN,

which she knows makes her as bad as him and Gladstone, but also has made a life-long quarrel between my son and I." Another to Lord Alfred Douglas was addressed to him as "you miserable creature," and ran: "What could be keener pain to have such a son as yourself. When quite a baby I cried over you the bitterest tears a man ever shed to have brought such a creature into the world."—Mr. Wilde denied that there was any truth in the accusation that his wife was seeking divorce. — Then came the next letter from Queensberry. It began, "You impertinent young jackanapes." — That was, interposed Mr. Carson, in reference to the reply which Lord Alfred sent his father by telegram. The telegram was put in and ran, "What a funny little man you are!"—Sir Edward continued the letter:—"You impertinent young jackanapes, if you come to me with any of your impertinence I shall give you the thrashing you richly deserve. The only excuse for you is that

YOU MUST BE CRAZY."

—The marquis then threatened to create a public scandal. Throughout the reading of these letters the scene in court was one of the most painful and astounding character. Sir Edward read on imperturbably, just in the tone he would have read a bill of costs. But the Marquis of Queensberry stood up, gazing alternately at Mr. Wilde in one corner, and at his son at the opposite end of the court. Every now and then he turned to the man in the witness box and

GROUND HIS TEETH

and shook his head at the witness in the most violent manner. Then when the more pathetic parts of the letters came the poor old nobleman had the greatest difficulty in restraining the tears that welled into his eyes, and forced him to bite his lips to keep them back. — Mr. Wilde said that such was the character of the letters; he took no notice of them. The acquaintanceship with Wood and the others was also gone into, and Mr. Wilde declared that, apart from the arrest of Parker upon a charge which the magistrate dismissed, nothing had ever come to his knowledge which led him to believe that any of the young fellows were living immoral or improper lives. Had it not been, he added, for the pressure put upon him by the Queensberry family he should have taken action against the marquis on account of the letters to Lord Alfred.—There the re-examination concluded. But for a few moments it was reopened, as Mr. Carson put in a postcard from Lord Alfred:—"As you have returned my letters unopened I am obliged to write on a postcard. I write to inform you that I treat your absurd threats with absolute indifference. Ever since your

EXHIBITION AT O.W.'S HOUSE

I have made a point of appearing with him at many public restaurants, and I shall continue to go to any of those places whenever I choose, and with whom I choose. I am of age, and my own master. You have disowned me at least a dozen times, and have very meanly deprived me of money. You have therefore no right over me either legal or moral. If O.W. was to prosecute you for libel in the criminal courts, you would get seven years' penal servitude for the outrageous libels. Much as I detest you I am anxious to avoid this for the sake of the family, but if you try to assault me I shall defend myself with a loaded revolver which I always carry, and I'll shoot you, or if he shoot you we should be completely justified, as we should be acting in self-defence against a violent and dangerous rough; and I think if you were dead not many people would miss you."—After this other terrible communication, the jury, too, wanted to put a question or two, and, after submitting them in writing to the judge, Mr. Wilde was asked whether the editor of the "Chameleon" was a personal friend. He was not; Mr. Wilde met him only once.—Was the "Chameleon" for private circulation? No, but only 100 copies were to be issued.—Was Mr. Wilde aware of the character of the story, "The Priest and the Acolyte?" He was not. It came upon him as a great shock.—Then at five minutes to three Mr. Wilde stepped down from the witness box and left the court.—Sir E. Clarke said the evidence for the prosecution was "closed for the present"—a qualification which Mr. Carson objected to.—His lordship said that, broadly put, the case for the prosecution must close now, but at his discretion he might admit some other evidence.—Mr. Carson then commenced his address to the jury by stating at once that Lord Queensberry did not withdraw any single allegation he had made, but

ABIDED BY WHAT HE HAD DONE,

at every hazard and at all cost. More than that if they believed the defence it was his bounden duty to do that which he had done in his efforts to save his son. Lord Queensberry was not actuated by malice. Mr. O. Wilde's character was known to him by his writings, and by the scandal at the Savoy, and it could be proved before the ending of the case that he had been seen in the company of men who were regarded as the most immoral men in London. Mr. Carson alluded more particularly to the man Taylor who had acted a sinister part. If Mr. Wilde's dealings with this person were harmless, why was not Taylor produced in support of his case? Witnesses, however, would be called who would show the kind of life which Taylor really led, and when the jury had heard all they would probably agree that Taylor was the pivot on which turned the whole of Mr. Wilde's associations. The prosecutor claimed a high place as an artist, his works could not be appreciated by the Philistine or the ignorant, so he told the court; and when a certain interpretation was placed on some passages from his works his reply was that no artist would put such an interpretation. Let the jury contrast this position with the Wilde had had to admit it himself.—Here came

A SENSATIONAL SURPRISE.

Sir Edward Clarke plucked Mr Carson by the gown, and the indulgence of the court was craved while counsel consulted. Mr. Wilde was not present in court, but he was in the building. Sir Edward and his junior, Mr. Mathews, had both been out of court for an interval before this surprise came. After a few moments' whispering, Mr. Carson resumed his seat and Sir Edward Clarke rose and said:—May I claim your lordship's indulgence while I interpose to make a statement, which, of course, is made under a feeling of very great responsibility? My learned friend, Mr. Carson, yesterday addressed the jury upon the question of the literature involved in this case, and upon the inferences to be drawn from the admissions made with regard to letters written by Mr. Oscar Wilde; and my friend began his address this morning by saying he hoped yesterday he had said enough in dealing with these topics to induce the jury to relieve him from the necessity of dealing in detail with the other issues in this case. I think it must have been present to your lordship's mind that those who represented Mr. Wilde in this case have before them a very terrible anxiety. They cannot conceal from themselves that the judgment that might be formed on that literature and upon the conduct which had been admitted might not improbably induce the jury to say that Lord Queensberry, in using the word "posing," was using a word for which there was sufficient justification to entitle the father who used those words under these circumstances to the utmost consideration, and to be relieved of a criminal charge in respect of his statement. And with this in our clear view, I and my learned friends associated with me in this matter, had to look forward to this, that a verdict given in favour of the defendant upon that part of the case might be interpreted outside as a conclusive finding with regard to all parts of the case, and the position in which we stood was this, that

WITHOUT EXPECTING A VERDICT

in this case, we should be going through day after day an investigation of matters of the most appalling character. Under these circumstances I hope your lordship will think I am taking the right course, which I take after communicating with Mr. Oscar Wilde. That is to say that, having regard to what has been referred to by my learned friend in respect of the matters connected with the literature and the letters, I feel he could not resist a verdict of not guilty in this case—not guilty having reference to the word "posing." Under these circumstances, I hope you will think I am not going beyond the bounds of my duty, and that I am doing something to save, to prevent, what would be a most terrible task, however it might close, if I now interpose and say on behalf of Mr. Oscar Wilde that I would ask to withdraw from the prosecution; and if you do not think that at this time of the case, and after what has taken place—if you do not think I ought to be allowed to do that on his behalf, I am prepared to submit to a verdict of not guilty, having reference, if to any part of the particulars at all, to that part of the particulars connected with the publication of "The Picture of Dorian Grey," and the publication of "The Chameleon." I trust that may make an end of the case.—Mr. Carson: I do not know that I have any right whatever to interfere in any way with this application my learned friend has made. I can only say, as far as Lord Queensberry is concerned, that if there is a plea of not guilty, a plea which involves that he has succeeded in his plea of justification, I am quite satisfied. Of course, my learned friend will admit we must succeed upon the plea in the manner in which he has stated, and that being so it rests entirely with your lordship as to whether the course suggested by my learned friend is to be taken.—His Lordship: Inasmuch as the prosecutor in this case is prepared

TO ACQUIESCE IN A VERDICT

of not guilty against the accused, I do not think it is any part of the function of the judge or jury to insist on going through prurient details which can have no bearing upon a matter already concluded by the assent of the prosecutor to an adverse verdict. But as to the jury putting any limitation upon the verdict of justification, the justification is one which is a justification of the charge, which is "posing as ——." If that is justified, it is justified; if it is not it is not; and the verdict of the jury upon it must be guilty or not guilty. I understand the prosecutor to assent to a verdict of not guilty. There can be no terms, and no limitations. The verdict must be guilty or not guilty. I understand him to assent to a verdict of not guilty, and, of course, the jury will return that.—Mr. Carson: Of course, the verdict will be that the plea of justification is proved, and that the words were published for the public benefit.—Sir E. Clarke: The verdict is "not guilty."—The Judge: The verdict is "not guilty," but it is arrived at by that process.—The

JURY THEN RETURNED A VERDICT

that the justification was proved, and that it was published for the public benefit, and that the accused was not guilty.—Mr. Carson said he presumed the costs of the defence would follow the verdict.—Mr. Gill and Mr. Mathews, with their long Old Bailey experience, reminded him that that followed by Act of Parliament.—There remained nothing further but the formal discharge of the accused. Long before this, congratulatory handshaking had been going on, the marquis leaning over the dock to reach the palms of his beaming friends. When the formal announcement of his discharge was made, the marquis left the dock amid cheers, which the officials of the court only half-heartedly attempted to stop.

WILDE ARRESTED.

After the verdict the public prosecutor was

him to lose, in a blaze of publicity, a case he would not otherwise have accepted. He acted unpaid, too, for Wilde's earnings soon dried up. Sherard tried to raise money for the legal costs from French sources. He repeatedly tried to persuade Sarah to mount *Salome* in Paris, or buy the copyright. Sarah sympathised, with floods of tears for poor, darling Oscar, but produced no money, and evaded Sherard's continuing importunity with transparent selfishness. Ross and Lord Ronald Gower left England, lest a general persecution of homosexuals begin, but Lord Alfred Douglas, who was in still greater danger, was loyal, tireless and fearless. His stupid obstinacy and childish family hatreds had done much to bring about the disaster, but now he stood by his friend, visiting him daily in gaol when bail had been refused, and looking after his affairs as best he could. As the trial approached and his danger increased, he finally gave way to Oscar's loving demand that he leave the country and save himself. But he did so unwillingly, and continued to champion his fallen friend, proudly regardless of the

fact that he would be marked for life as the participant figure in a major scandal.

Constance left Tite Street, and withdrew the boys from school. Like Oscar, she was stupidly bewildered by the failure of the palmist's predictions, and hopefully consulted the fashionable sybil again. She was coming to depend increasingly on her cousins, the Adrian Hopes, for advice and support. The drawback to this was that they detested Oscar, whom they referred to as 'that beast'. They were to do everything in their respectable and cold-hearted power to drive a rift between husband and wife.

On 26th April the trial began. Oscar still had enough fight in him to make a rousing defence of 'the love that dare not speak its name', suggesting that the love of an older man for a younger was historically, and indeed scripturally, sanctioned, and was particularly likely to occur in the cases of fine, creative spirits. Max Beerbohm, going to support his friend from the public gallery, was impressed with the performance by a man who had been refused bail, and had suffered a month's unaccustomed imprisonment. Max wrongly assumed that Oscar's bearing was bound to lead to an acquittal. In the light of the fact that the 'panthers' were all happily in court, enjoying the opportunity to give evidence against their former patron, and at the same time trying to solicit new trade from likely prospects who came to hear the trial, it is astonishing that Oscar even persuaded the jury to disagree.

left Contemporary press coverage of Wilde's action against the Marquess. Oscar's arrest is noted at the conclusion of the account.

below Holloway Prison: still a men's prison when Wilde was confined there in the 1890s.

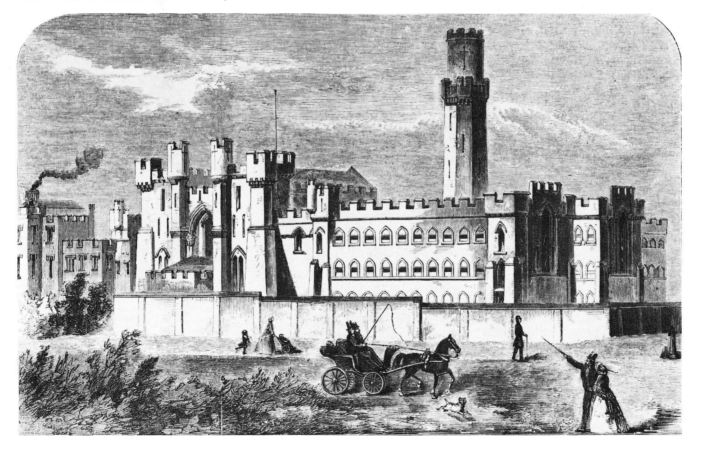

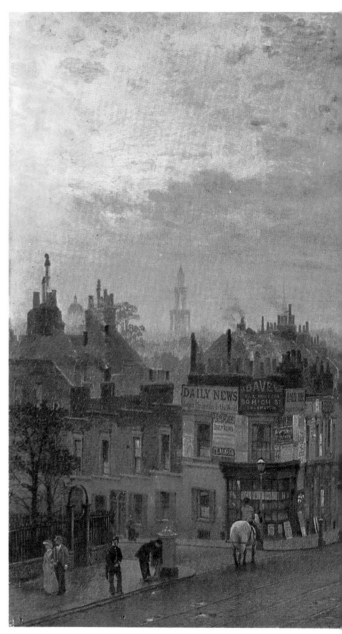

above left The High Art Maiden, a popular song of 1887. By this time Oscar Wilde and Constance Lloyd had been married for three years and were the parents of two sons. But Constance, as a young mother, could not aspire to the aesthetic pretensions satirized here and spent much of her time without her husband's company.

above For the majority of Londoners in the eighties life was very far removed from the elegance of *The Woman's World* and Oscar Wilde's comedies. John O'Connor's *Horse Trams on Pentonville Hill* evokes the smoky bustle of working-class life. The London Museum.

right Joseph Solomon's *Conversation Piece*, 1884. This picture captures very well the heavy lushness of wealthy late-Victorian society. Leighton House, London.

If that lack of a verdict had been allowed to stand, and the case discontinued, justice might now be seen to have been done. The shock of public failure and a month's incarceration was no more than Oscar Wilde deserved. He had resorted to a legal system he knew to be unjust to win by perjury a harsh punishment for an unbalanced enemy. But from now on, Wilde was the victim, and the godly arrayed against him proved themselves loathsome.

The Liberal government, knowing that Wilde was widely regarded as a Liberal sympathiser, may have felt it politically necessary to pursue the prosecution vigorously. Scabrous rumours were circulating to the effect that figures as high as cabinet circles were compromised by Wilde's and Queensberry's letters. The Home Secretary, Herbert Asquith, may have been embarrassed by the fact that he and his fellow 'Souls' – a group of smart, cultivated young politicians – had numbered Wilde among their friends. The Solicitor-General's wife's nephew was in fact homosexually acquainted with Wilde, and had been seen in bed with him by hotel servants. The government appointed the Solicitor-General to prosecute, and he not only disregarded Carson's personal request to him to 'let up on the fellow', but directed the case against Wilde with such vigour, suggesting personal animus, that the mild Clarke was led to protest.

A peculiarly nasty legal decision was that Wilde and Alfred Taylor should be tried together and jointly for 'conspiracy'. This meaningless charge was brought out, as is so often the case, to divert the course of justice to a political end. When the charge was thrown out at Wilde's first trial, a dubious arrangement to have Taylor and Wilde tried consecutively before the same court was set up to replace the pleasure of seeing the playwright in the dock with the perverts' pander.

Taylor had behaved with quite unpredictable courage. When he was offered immunity from prosecution if he would testify against Wilde, the silly, irresponsible organiser of meetings between twittering transvestites and robust young grooms refused point-blank to accept so dishonourable a deal. He could be both used and punished as a co-defendant, and in the 1890s he disappeared in the darkness of universal opprobrium when he was sent down with Wilde. It is now clear that he was one of the few men who evinced courage, honour and decency during the affair.

After his first trial, Wilde had to be released on bail. With characteristic vindictiveness, the authorities set this absurdly high, at £5,000. Percy Douglas and the Rev. Stewart Headlam stood surety; the latter hardly knew Wilde, but saw it as his Christian duty to help a man who was being

martyred. Neither surety could easily have met the cost of broken bail, but both sensed the evil mood of the country, and urged Wilde to escape to France.

When Oscar Wilde was released on bail from Holloway Prison, he was driven to seek shelter with his mother at Oakley Street. Queensberry had hired a gang of ruffians to follow him from hotel to hotel, threatening to create a rumpus in any establishment whose management allowed the notorious sodomite to stay there.

Life at Oakley Street, however, was almost intolerable. Willie had washed up there, after a short-lived marriage to an American millionairess. The first Mrs Willie Wilde had a shady background. Her mother was reputed to have kept a brothel and – almost equally questionable in the 1890s – there was African blood in the family. She herself was the widow of a perfectly respectable American financier, and found it impossible to live with Willie, who saw her as the heaven-sent opening to a sea of whisky. Now, drunken and divorced, Willie was insisting that his brother was an Irish gentleman, and would stay and face the music. 'My poor, dear brother,' said Oscar on hearing that Willie was defending him all over London, 'could compromise a steam-engine.' As Willie's classic mode of defence was to assert that Oscar was not a man of bad character – you could trust him with a woman anywhere – this may well have been true.

Speranza, too, set her face against Oscar's escaping his second trial. She promised that her affection would be unshaken, whatever its outcome. But if he ran away he would cease to be her son.

Sherard, paying a flying visit to Oakley Street was hardly more encouraging. When Oscar gained a little histrionic relief by moaning, 'Why have you brought me no poison from Paris?' Sherard unkindly told him exactly how to manufacture prussic acid if he really wanted it. It was a relief when the Leversons descended on Oakley Street and took Oscar away to live secretly in their nursery until the trial.

To their house came Ellen Terry, heavily veiled, but still affectionate. She brought a bunch of violets, and a note of encouragement from herself and Irving. The whole business had been a little mysterious to Ellen, who never quite understood what Oscar was supposed to have been doing. Another leading actress took a more simply robust attitude to the scandal flying around London: 'I don't care what they do,' said Mrs Patrick Campbell, 'as long as they don't do it in the streets and frighten the horses.'

Frank Harris urged Oscar to go to France. He may have offered to accompany him, though it is implausible in the highest degree that, as he later claimed, he borrowed a steam yacht in which to make the dash for freedom. A lady from Wimbledon, Miss Adela Schuster, whose parents' dinner-table had often been enlivened by Oscar, sent him £1,000 for his necessary expenses. Oscar gave it to Leverson, who agreed to manage his affairs. Unfortunately, on the way to court Oscar absent-mindedly agreed that Leverson could re-imburse himself from this money for at least some of the £500 he had lent him a couple of months earlier.

And so, on 20 May, came the second trial, before the hostile Mr Justice Wills. The evidence was clear enough. Landladies had wondered about goings-on. Servants at the Savoy Hotel had noticed curious visitors and stained sheets when Oscar stayed there. The boys appeared and told their squalid stories again. The evidence against Taylor and Wilde, taken in succession before a hostile court, left little hope for either man.

Taylor was found guilty first. Queensberry enjoyed this foretaste of triumph, and sent a gloating telegram to his son Percy's wife:

To Lady Douglas: Must congratulate on verdict. Cannot on Percy's appearance. Looked like a dug up corpse. Fear too much madness of kissing. Taylor guilty. Wilde's turn tomorrow.
QUEENSBERRY.

This communication led to a brawl in the street when father and son met, and both were bound over to keep the peace.

The morrow brought verdict and sentence. The judge passed the severest sentence the law allowed – two years hard labour – and added the unnecessary and unpleasant comment that in his opinion it was totally inadequate.

'And I?' cried Oscar from the dock. 'May I say nothing, my lord?' He was allowed to say nothing.

Outside in the streets a few prostitutes kicked up their skirts in a gesture of contempt towards all posh queers. 'He'll have his hair cut regular *now*!' shouted one. They reflected accurately the meanly triumphant attitude of respectable society, which rejoiced to see the irritating artist brought down. Short hair and militaristic imperialism could now become the pattern for British life. Wilde was to be forgotten, if possible. The christian name 'Oscar' was to fall into almost total disuse. George Alexander went on making money by *The Importance of Being Earnest*, but with good British and Victorian hypocrisy he took the author's name off the posters and programmes. Soon he closed its run. *An Ideal Husband* had closed earlier. Lane lost no time in calling in all Wilde's works from the booksellers. A disgraced man must not be allowed a living. Society, having enjoyed a banquet of scandalous exposure, now took its customary dessert of smugness and cruelty.

Mr Justice Wills. His benevolent appearance before cartoonist Spy was misleading: he enthusiastically made himself the instrument of Oscar Wilde's public martyrdom.

above Peacock Garden wallpaper, designed
by Walter Crane, 1889. Crane was a disciple
of William Morris, and one of the illustrators
of *The Happy Prince*.

left Avon chintz wallpaper of the same period,
designed by William Morris.

right Charles Ricketts' design for *The Sphinx*,
1893. British Museum.

THE SPHINX BY OSCAR WILDE

MELANCHOLIA

WITH DECORATIONS BY CHARLES RICKETTS
LONDON MDCCCXCIV
ELKIN MATHEWS AND JOHN LANE . AT THE SIGN OF THE BODLEY HEAD.

PRISON

'The present prison system seems almost to have for its aim the wrecking and the destruction of the mental faculties.'

The prisoner was hurried down the steps from the dock to the cells. Two days later he was taken out, handcuffed, and taken in a horse-drawn van to Pentonville.

Now started his utter humiliation. He was weighed and measured. His personal possessions were taken from him. He was stripped and put into a filthy bath of disinfectant. A damp brown rag was handed to him for use as a towel. He was given a medical examination and certified fit for 'light labour' – picking oakum and sewing mailbags. He was given his cheap, ill-cut prison clothing, stamped with the government's broad arrow. His hair was cropped.

In his cell, as the law prescribed, was a 'hard bed'. It was of bare planks, and induced, as was intended, wretched insomnia. He received, as the law prescribed, 'hard food' – gruel, dry bread, greasy bacon, beans, fatty cocoa. The unaccustomed coarseness of the diet gave him, like most other prisoners, chronic diarrhoea.

From his cell the water closet had been removed. Prisoners had been known to tap messages to each other along the plumbing. In its place was a chamber-pot. The cell stank overnight, and the prisoner found in himself the generosity to feel sorry for the warders who had to enter a succession of stinking cells every morning.

The prisoner was allowed one book a week. This was the most terrible deprivation for a cultivated man. Chain-smoker though he had been, he found it far easier to reconcile himself to the lack of tobacco.

The prisoner was utterly starved of the company of his equals. It would be twenty months before he met a warder whom he could accept as a friend. The chaplain was a sanctimonious ass. 'Did you have morning prayers in your house?' he asked. 'I am sorry. I fear not,' was the prisoner's courteous reply. 'You see where you are now,' said the ordained fool, whose monthly visits were intended to be the

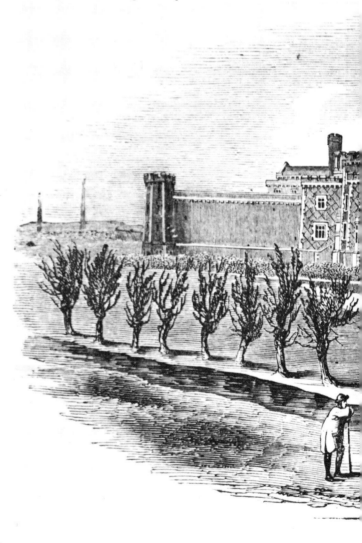

Reading Gaol: setting of Wilde's greatest suffering as well as his greatest poem.

prisoner's sole opportunity to converse with an educated man.

In July the prisoner was transferred to Wandsworth. One day he fainted in chapel, falling and bruising his ear. The doctor merely accused him of malingering, and by his negligence permitted an abscess to develop which, in turn, led to a perforated ear-drum and partial deafness. With some justification, the son of Sir William Wilde wrote that prison doctors were 'as a class, ignorant men'. What ultimately appalled him was not his own suffering, but the unspeakable inhumanity of the prison doctor in Reading, who permitted a half-witted convict to be flogged for petty infringements of trivial rules he was incapable of understanding.

The removal to Reading came in November. Reports in the press that Oscar Wilde's health was suffering under the prison regimen had aroused the Home Office, and he was transferred to a prison where he could vary his oakum-picking with some outdoor gardening and light work repairing books in the library. The move came without warning, and on 13 November Oscar Wilde found himself handcuffed and guarded on the centre platform at Clapham Junction, waiting for a train. It was unbearably humiliating to the proud and sensitive Oscar to be stared at, recognised, and mocked by passing travellers.

The governor of Reading Gaol, Major Henry Isaacson, was a severe and stupid martinet. He boasted that he was 'knocking the nonsense out of Wilde', and took pleasure in punishing him. But the regimen of Reading was healthier than that of the London prisons. Wilde had lost twenty-two pounds since his incarceration began. Now he began to put on a little weight again.

In May 1896 Trooper C. T. Wooldridge joined the remand prisoners in the exercise yard. He was on trial for having cut his young wife's throat in a fit of jealousy. He was found guilty in June, and while public petitions for his reprieve were prepared and refused, the prisoners watched the sombre preparations for his execution in the gaol. Wilde experienced the tension that built up in the prison as the day of execution approached, and it was to give him material for his finest poem:

> We sewed the sacks, we broke the stones,
>   We turned the dusty drill:
> We banged the tins, and bawled the hymns,

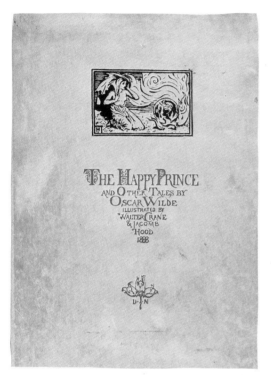

The cover for *The Happy Prince*, 1888.
Victoria and Albert Museum.

Robert de Montesquiou, leader of the
Paris aesthetes, occupied a position similar
to that of Wilde's in London. But he was
outwardly more circumspect and loathed
Wilde – he took care to avoid meeting him
because of his reputation.

right Robert Ross at the age of twenty-one, a
portrait by William Rothenstein. In the
collection of Sir John Rothenstein.

Constance in 1894.

The Marquess of Queensberry,
as seen by Max Beerbohm in 1894.

And sweated on the mill:
But in the heart of every man
Terror was lying still.

Prison was intensifying Wilde's view of Christ as the first poet, the arch-romantic, the sympathetic figure whose sacrifice could provide a satisfying curtain to any tragedy, including his own and Wooldridge's.

The Chaplain does not kneel to pray
Beside his unhallowed grave,
Nor mark it with that blessed cross
That Christ for sinners gave,
Because the man is one of those
Whom Christ came down to save.

But this calm view was realised after he had left prison. In July 1896 Oscar Wilde seriously feared that he would be unbalanced for life, and he wrote two desperate, unsuccessful petitions to the Home Secretary, praying for his early release. He was so emotionally disturbed that he was willing to accept the condemnatory view of his nature which had led him to prison in England, and, he seemed to suggest, might well have led him to an asylum.

'The Petitioner is now keenly conscious of the fact that while the three years preceding his arrest were from the intellectual point of view the most brilliant years of his life . . . still that during the entire time he was suffering from the most horrible form of erotomania.' He was echoing poor, bewildered Constance, who told Sherard, 'He has been mad these last three years.'

The marriage was effectively over. Constance's relatives, friends and solicitors all advised her to petition for divorce. She changed her name to Holland, and fled to the continent to avoid the screaming publicity of the trials and sentence. But she was still fond of Oscar, and loyal, by her lights (though understanding she could not be); she came back to see him in prison and talk about the future. She was appalled by the interview. Prisoner and visitor were locked in separate boxes, with wire netting over the holes through which they could talk to each other. Warders stood between them to censor their conversation.

In the spring of 1896 she made the journey from Genoa to London in order that she personally might give her husband the distressing news that his mother had died. Speranza had contracted bronchitis during the winter, and in her enfeebled condition after her son's arrest and conviction she had no hope of recovery. Wilde was touched by his wife's kindness and gentleness, and for all the intolerable boredom marriage had inflicted on him it was through no wish of his that they became estranged.

right Toulouse-Lautrec was in London just before the last trial, and talked to Wilde the evening before. He executed this study immediately afterwards.

below La Goulue dancing, by Toulouse-Lautrec, 1895. Oscar Wilde is the figure in the foreground (back to the artist) wearing a fawn overcoat. Louvre.

below and right Art Nouveau. William de
Morgan's peacock dish is dated 1898; an
earlier example is *The Pelican*, a pastel panel
of 1881 by Edward Burne-Jones now in the
William Morris Gallery, Walthamstow.

bottom Walter Spindler's painting, *Sarah
Bernhardt in the rôle of Ghismonda*, 1895.
Sarah professed enormous sympathy for
Oscar when he was convicted and imprisoned
but actually did nothing to help him, then or
later.

127

The difficulty between them was a question of
money. With Wilde behind bars, Queensberry was
still not satisfied, and to recover his costs of £677
incurred in the libel proceedings, he started an action
to have his enemy bankrupted and his assets seized.
Wilde had been told that the Douglas family would
shoulder the costs: in fact they came up with a
beggarly £50. When Wilde's house and goods were
set against his debts, he was insolvent by several
thousand pounds. His income was derived from the
royalties on his books and plays but this had dried up
very quickly after his conviction. The sale of the
Tite Street house and its contents failed to realise
even its actual value: Wilde's priceless collection of
signed presentation copies of first editions from the
leading writers of England and Europe was split up,
and some of his manuscripts were actually stolen.
His one remaining asset was his marriage settlement,
according to which Constance's estate was to pay
him £200 a year in the event of her death. This was
of little value, as she seemed likely to outlive him,
but the creditors wanted it sold. Constance's legal
advisers urged her to buy it so that she might retain
unquestioned control of the children. Wilde was
agreeable, but the friends who were handling his
affairs thought it better that they should buy in the
settlement on his behalf. Constance assumed that
they were acting on her husband's instructions, and
felt that this proved him utterly unreliable.
Although she drew up a new legal agreement by
which she committed herself to paying him £150 a
year as a substitute for the original settlement, they
never met again. Worst of all, from Wilde's point of
view, the officious bungling which had offended
Constance led her to take legal steps to prevent him
from having access to his children.

But those friends had proved too loyal, and worked
too hard, if wrong-headedly, on his behalf for Oscar
to bear malice. Robbie Ross and his friend the
translator and art connoisseur More Adey had tried

to meet Oscar's needs during his imprisonment, and Oscar himself felt that Adey's solicitor was really responsible for misleading them. Robbie's loyalty touched Oscar deeply when he was taken from prison to appear in the Bankruptcy Court. A crowd had gathered to watch his rapid progress in handcuffs from the police van, across the pavement, and into the courtroom. Ross placed himself at the front of the crowd in order to take his hat off to his friend as he went by; a simple, unobtrusive gesture, but the largest fillip Oscar's morale received during the first year of his imprisonment.

Robert Sherard, too, had proved loyal. Although in the years of his success Oscar had found Sherard increasingly boring, and had treated him in an off-hand manner that distressed the would-be disciple, Sherard did not now reproach him but came and visited him in prison. He noticed that Oscar was particularly embarrassed by the impossibility of shaving daily, and tried to cover his scrubby chin with a handkerchief. Like Constance, Sherard was unable to understand homosexuality as anything but a temporary mental aberration, and he believed that Alfred Douglas had 'infected' Wilde. This led him to join with Robbie Ross, who for quite other reasons wanted Oscar to drop Bosie, and reinstate himself as the nearest and dearest friend. Constance, too, believed that Douglas was a 'beast', and put a special clause in her final agreement with Oscar which, in effect, debarred him from associating with Douglas on pain of losing his small income from her.

Under the traumatic conditions of prison life, Oscar was easily suggestible. He had left court still deeply in love with Bosie. Now he came to believe that the young man's headstrong selfishness was responsible for all his suffering. He was irritated when a solicitor's clerk, visiting him during the bankruptcy proceedings, passed on the secret and confidential message, 'Prince Fleur-de-Lys wishes to be remembered to you.' The artificial pseudonym seemed cruelly out of place in prison. Yet it was entirely in key with the letters he had been writing Bosie immediately before his conviction, and Bosie could no longer contact him openly.

When Ross and Sherard announced that Douglas proposed publishing his letters from Wilde in a French journal, it seemed like the ultimate betrayal: a showy and dangerous parade of their relationship. Oscar forbade it outright. Yet Douglas had only intended to quote from the letters in the course of an article protesting strongly against his friend's imprisonment. He was violently loyal, though almost helpless, and not without reason he came to feel that Oscar's mind was being mysteriously poisoned against him.

Frank Harris was another true friend. He visited Wilde twice in Reading, having first been to see Evelyn Ruggles-Brise, the Chairman of the Prison Commission. On Harris's report that Wilde was looking older and suffering from the lack of intellectual stimulation, more books were made available to the prisoner.

Following official hints, Harris also tried to organise a petition of distinguished writers on Wilde's behalf. Meredith, who would have carried real weight, turned him down, as did almost all other writers of note. Shaw had once found Wilde to be the only distinguished British writer willing to sign a petition on behalf of some Chicago anarchists (against whose death sentence Harris had also protested in the *Fortnightly Review*). Now G.B.S. was perfectly willing to lend support to Wilde, but he warned Harris that he and the Reverend Stewart Headlam were 'notorious cranks' whose socialist signatures might do more harm than good. Professor Tyrrell of Dublin signed out of loyalty to his old pupil. And quiet sympathy, taking the form of gifts of books for the prisoner also came from Max Beerbohm, Will Rothenstein the artist, and the brothers A.E. and Laurence Housman. But for want of great names and all their efforts the petition failed.

Harris may have achieved something useful, however, if he reported back the profoundly unfavourable impression Major Isaacson made on him. At any rate, Isaacson was transferred to another post, and for his last six months in Reading Wilde enjoyed the civilized governorship of Major J.O. Nelson. Punishments throughout the prison fell by half. Wilde was given writing materials and allowed to embark on the long letter to Lord Alfred Douglas which became known as *De Profundis*. It was a therapeutic exercise, in which he poured out all his bitterness, self-hatred, hurt vanity, and guilt. At times it wept with hysterical penitence. At others it hurled lacerating reproaches at Douglas. Before it was finished, the tone began to change. Wilde began to consider the possibility of a calm and distant friendship with Douglas in the future, and it had obviously done him a lot of good to write out his bile and misery. He told Robbie Ross to take charge of the letter on his release, and have two copies made before sending the original to Douglas.

At the very end of the sentence a kindly warder was added to the humane governor. Thomas Martin was willing to smuggle biscuits in to the hungry prisoners under his charge, provided they scrupulously picked up any tell-tale crumbs. He passed on his daily paper to Oscar Wilde, and took the even greater risk of buying him the literary journals he requested. Their relationship is best summed up in one hasty exchange of clandestine notes:

'My dear friend, What have I to write about except that if you had been an officer in Reading Prison a year ago my life would have been much happier. Everyone tells me I am looking better – and happier.

That is because I have a good friend who gives me the *Chronicle*, and *promises* me ginger biscuits!'

O.W.

In reply, Martin quickly pencilled,

'Your ungrateful I done more than promise.'

Martin believed that the governor was also breaking the rules in the interest of this unusually sensitive prisoner. And certainly the last two months of prison were far less terrible than the first year, which had truly broken Wilde's spirit. Martin was unable to believe the tearfulness which visitors reported of his charge. But many utterly reliable observers noted Wilde's uncontrollable tendency to break down after his imprisonment.

Oscar Wilde, convict number C.3.3, was popular with his fellow-prisoners. They recognised that he was suffering more severely than they, and respected his refusal to put on airs. He later referred to himself jocularly as 'a member of the criminal classes', but in fact he was deeply moved by the humanity and consideration prisoners showed one another. As his release approached he prepared to play his part in a continuing cycle of mutual assistance, with small monetary gifts for released inmates, and introductions to potential employers. He was, however, embarrassed when one convict kept attracting his attention by using masonic signs, and asking him as a brother-mason to use social influence to obtain his release. He managed to avoid the mason by adopting 'black goggles' in the exercise yard, presumably with the governor's connivance.

If Wilde was one of the first middle-class prisoners to discover that convicted felons may be sympathetic human beings, he was also one of the few to see that the same was true of warders. They too were trapped in the brutalising prison system, and it was laws beyond their control that made many screws seem severe. Of course, there were some bullying brutes among them; but he never felt as strongly about the uneducated warders as he did about the supposedly educated doctors. And to kind warders he returned kindness. With his literary skill, he provided apt entries for newspaper competitions, which enabled one newly-married warder to win a tea-service, while another collected a grand piano!

As the last weeks of imprisonment crept on, Oscar Wilde's mind was occupied with two questions. What was he going to live on after his release? And what could he do for his fellow victims?

Robbie Ross in his maturity.

THE FINAL ACT

'Everyone is born a king, and most people die in exile, like most kings.'

On a morning in May 1897 a smart pill-box brougham drove up to a house in Bloomsbury, and put down a fashionably dressed couple. They were shown into a room decorated with William Morris wallpaper and curtains, after the fashion of the early 1880s. They were a little apprehensive about the meeting that was due to take place.

A tall, elegantly-dressed man, with his hair waved, a flower in his buttonhole, and a cigarette in his hand, came in, talking and laughing.

'Sphinx,' cried Oscar, 'how marvellous of you to know exactly the right hat to wear at seven o'clock in the morning to meet a friend who has been away! You can't have got up, you must have sat up.' The Leversons were relieved to find that their friend's exquisite tact was unchanged. They also noticed that he looked thinner and healthier than he had in 1895.

A message was sent to the Jesuit Fathers in Farm Street, where Wilde hoped to go into retreat for six months. Other visitors arrived: the young solicitor and his wife whose marriage had been financed from the profits of *Lady Windermere's Fan*. The house was the Reverend Stewart Headlam's: at six o'clock he and More Adey had fetched Oscar from Pentonville, where he had been transferred from Reading the previous day.

Conversation was light. Oscar was delightfully amusing about prison, until an answer was received from Farm Street. It refused his request, and at last the strain proved too much, and he broke down.

In the afternoon, Wilde and Adey left for Newhaven, where they caught the night-train for France. At Dieppe, Robbie Ross and Reggie Turner met them, and a short holiday began. It was impossible for Oscar to sustain any anger with these friends for the way in which they had mishandled some of his affairs. They had given him clothes and books. Turner, who always loved surprising friends with perfectly chosen gifts, had delighted him with a dressing-case whose silver contents were engraved with the initials 'S.M.' For it had been decided that Oscar was to live incognito in France as 'Sebastian

Melmoth'. With something like delight in his own notoriety, Oscar wrote to the Sphinx, 'Reggie Turner is staying here under the name "Robert Ross". Robbie under the name "Reginald Turner". It is better they should not use their own names.'

In Dieppe the French actor Lugnë-Poè, who had produced *Salome* while Wilde was in prison, came to pay his compliments. From his cell, Oscar had been profoundly impressed by the fact that his work could be performed in Paris while everything of his was tabooed in London. Although he had once hoped that he might be able to live in England and take up the broken threads of his literary career, he now came to realise that continental exile offered the only future for him.

The four friends toured northern France, looking for somewhere for Oscar to live. Eventually they fixed on Berneval-sur-Mer, a few miles from Dieppe. Then Turner and Adey returned to London, while Ross stayed to help Oscar settle in. After a few days Ross, too, had to leave, and Oscar Wilde began the life of a secluded alien writer in a small French village. He started work on his long poem *The Ballad of Reading Gaol*.

At first the life seemed quite pleasant. Monsieur Melmoth was popular in the village, especially when he celebrated Queen Victoria's Diamond Jubilee by giving a fête for the local children, and presenting them all with the toy accordions and trumpets they asked for. And from his small stock of money there were presents to be made to friends who had left prison. A total of twenty-two pounds was distributed by Ross among ex-prisoners at Wilde's request.

From Reading came the news that Martin had been dismissed for giving a biscuit to the youngest of three children who had been gaoled for rabbit-snaring. Wilde payed the children's fines to secure their release, and wrote a powerful letter to the *Daily Chronicle*. In it he attacked the evil of incarcerating children under fourteen, spoke with justified horror of the flogging of the half-witted convict A.2.11, exposed the evils of silent and solitary confinement, and put forward unpalatable facts about food and living conditions. It was one of his finest pieces of writing. No time was wasted in mental acrobatics; no paradox or epigram distracted attention from the clear, unsentimental humanity of the writer. He was fair to the warders, but he used his perceptive intelligence to show how the system failed:

'People nowadays do not understand what cruelty is.... Ordinary cruelty is simply stupidity. It is the entire want of imagination. It is the result in our days of stereotyped systems of hard-and-fast rules, and of stupidity.... The people who uphold the system have excellent intentions.... It is supposed that because a thing is the rule it is right.' The utter repudiation of any form of cruelty remained the central feature of Oscar Wilde's moral personality.

A year later, when a Prison Reform Bill was before Parliament, he returned to the subject. This time he pointed out to *Daily Chronicle* readers that an increase in prison inspectors would not make life any the more bearable for prisoners, as irksome rules would only be the more scrupulously observed. Wilde's two letters on prison reform constitute a notable contribution to the literature of penology.

A few friends visited him when they were in Dieppe. Ernest Dowson brought with him Charles Conder, an impoverished artist who painted exquisite fans, and according to Oscar was skilled at wheedling 100 francs for them from people like himself who would willingly have given 300! It was rumoured that Dowson insisted on taking Oscar to a Dieppe brothel, in the hope that this would alter

The distinguished French actor and director, Aurelien Marie Lugnë-Poè, who staged the first production of *Salome* and created the role of Herod; this was while Oscar was in Reading Gaol. Lugnë-Poè went to pay his respects as soon as he heard that the author was in France.

below Dieppe in the nineteenth century.

his sexual tastes. Rumour went on to say that the expedition was a failure: Oscar said it was 'like dining off cold mutton'.

Dowson also introduced Wilde to his publisher, Leonard Smithers. This was important, as Lane was now refusing to issue any books by the infamous sodomite, and no other reputable publisher would be willing to take *The Ballad*. But Smithers published undisguised pornography under the counter, and was always happy to take the dangerous *fin-de-siècle* work that other publishers sheered off. And it was agreed that he should publish Oscar's poem when it was complete.

Aubrey Beardsley visited Dieppe with his mother and sister, and tried to meet Oscar as little as possible. He could not avoid him altogether, but he did once scurry down a sidestreet to avoid a chance encounter. 'It was *lâche* of Aubrey,' was Oscar's tolerant comment.

At first a tentative, secretive correspondence was started with Bosie. Ross, Sherard and Lady Queensberry all opposed any renewal of the friendship. But life at Berneval became lonely: all his adult life Oscar Wilde had been a man of the cities, easily bored with country retirement. It was impossible for Bosie to come to Berneval, as Oscar had seen a man who might have been a detective hired by Queensberry in the village. But the two finally met at Rouen, and spent the day walking hand-in-hand together. Oscar was ecstatically happy, and made immediate arrangements to go and live at Naples with Bosie.

They spent an expensive week at a Naples hotel, and then moved to the Villa Giudice, Posilippo. Robbie wrote angry letters, and was flatly told that the reunion was inevitable. Reggie was asked to 'stick up for us ... and be nice'. Sherard was firmly told that his indiscreet condemnation of the liaison had re-echoed from Paris to Naples, and exposed him 'to rebuke and contempt'.

Then Wilde and Douglas called in the local witch to rid the villa of rats, got down to working on *The Ballad* together, and for the last three months of 1897 lived a happy companionate life.

It lasted no longer because the women held the purse-strings. Constance's Deed of Arrangement entitled her to stop Oscar's limited funds if he associated with Bosie, and Lady Queensberry prepared to cut off Bosie's allowance. There was nothing the two could do but bow to the inevitable, and separate. Bosie insisted that his mother should pay Oscar £200 – the most she could afford – towards the legal costs that he agreed the Queensberry family owed him. But in return he had to agree that they would never again stay under the same roof. He left Oscar in Naples, so sad and miserable that

he was soon trying to curry favour with Robbie by claiming that Bosie had sponged off him, and deserted as soon as his money ran out. This was quite untrue; but for the rest of his life Oscar was to be fretted by the want of money, and unreasonable with those who met any of his expenses.

Money led to an embarrassing end of communications with the Sphinx. Of the £1,000 Miss Schuster had put at Wilde's disposal, little over £100 remained when he left gaol. Solicitors' fees had eaten much of the money, and there were other legitimate items. But Oscar was furious to find that the largest single item deducted was £250 with which Ernest Leverson had reimbursed himself for part of his earlier loan. If Leverson chose to be his creditor, then, Wilde felt, he should join the queue waiting outside the Bankruptcy Court. But Leverson, though he talked of another possible loan, refused to return the money, as things were 'very tight in the city'. Wilde interpreted this to mean that Leverson had gambled away his £250 on the Stock Exchange, and he may not have been far wrong. Leverson was a compulsive gambler, whose marked preference for roulette tables rather than domesticity had led to unhappiness in the Sphinx's marriage from its outset. Whether or not Oscar knew of this strain, which was ultimately to lead to reduced circumstances and a separation for the Leversons, delicacy necessitated his gently diminishing his correspondence with a lady whose husband, he felt, had robbed him.

He returned to Paris. *The Ballad of Reading Gaol*, published over the pseudonym C.3.3, was an immense success. Smithers, used to handling books of limited appeal, had far too few copies printed to meet the demand. A French translation kept Wilde

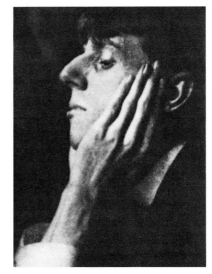

top Posilippo, on the Bay of Naples. Oscar and Bosie spent a short but idyllic period together at the Villa Giudice.

top right Oscar Wilde, the English tourist in Rome, alternately seeing the sights, collecting Papal blessings, and picking up attractive youths.

above The shabby life of the cafés. *Oscar Wilde au cabaret, rue de Dunkerque,* by Jean Matet.

above right Aubrey Beardsley near the end of his life.

before the public eye in Paris. But he disappointed French friends who expected him to share their Anglophobia as the Boer War smouldered into open fighting. He proved to be staunchly patriotic. And he disappointed English friends who hoped *The Ballad* heralded further writing. His spirit was broken, and for the remaining two years he drifted.

He drifted to the island of Sicily to stay at Taormina with Baron von Gloeden, whose hobby was photographing naked peasant boys. He drifted to Gland in Switzerland, with a young Englishman named Harold Mellor who had been expelled from Harrow for seducing the cricket captain. He found Mellor a mean host, serving cheap wine. He drifted to the south of France with Frank Harris, and amusedly watched George Alexander cycle past him with a sickly smile but no open greeting. Sarah, by contrast, greeted him with tears, kisses, and rapture. He drifted to Rome and made a point of repeatedly receiving the Papal blessing at public audiences. But still he would not commit himself to Catholicism. Everywhere he went he picked up beautiful young men, and he told his sympathetic friends in England about them, and sent some of them to London to share their talents with Robbie and Reggie.

He returned to Paris, and found Bosie there. They saw a lot of each other, and shared young men. Robert Sherard had become intolerably boring, and Wilde and Douglas, who had suffered the humiliation of being asked to leave hotels at the height of the scandal, now had the pleasure of saving the moralistic Sherard from being banned from a bar where he had tried to start an anti-Semitic brawl. The Dreyfus affair was dominating Paris life and Sherard was a profound anti-Dreyfusard. Wilde was not; but he was not much interested in the innocent Jewish captain who had been disgraced on the trumped-up charge of betraying military secrets. The villainous Count Esterhazy, who had forged evidence against Dreyfus, was far more exciting, and Wilde thoroughly enjoyed a private dinner to which Esterhazy brought his blowzy mistress, and at which he almost confessed his guilt. The young Serge Diaghilev was a more predictable companion for Wilde; but he was in Paris at this time only as a rich connoisseur, not as impresario of the *Ballets Russes*.

Oscar Wilde had fallen into the shabby life of the cafés. His letters to all his friends begged for money. He lived in respectable, ordinary hotels, and lamented Ross's refusal to allow him the money for an apartment where he could keep young men overnight. He drank more and more absinthe, and grew fat on cheap food. He watched the world go by.

He succeeded in swindling Frank Harris (no mean feat!) by selling him the scenario for a play. When Harris wrote it up, and prepared to have it produced, he found that Wilde had sold the scenario to several other people, who had to be bought off. Oscar managed to be morally indignant, claiming that Harris had crudely cut off a useful source of income in the scenario that he could have gone on selling to gullible people for years.

Constance died. He was surprised, for he had not known that she was suffering from a serious spinal infection. He was grieved, for dilatory hesitation on both sides had prevented their meeting. He felt shamed when he saw her grave, with no mention of his name. He would have been quite rightly outraged had he known that Constance's virtuous family were proceeding to treat his sons as rather shameful poor relations, and imposing an unloved childhood on them.

Aubrey Beardsley died of consumption, a penitent Catholic, begging Smithers to destroy his openly erotic *Lysistrata* prints. Willie Wilde died after a second marriage, and the almost complete forfeiture of Oscar's good-will by his losing (or pawning) the favourite fur coat of American days, which had been

THE YELLOW BOOK
AN ILLUSTRATED QUARTERLY.

PRICE FIVE SHILLINGS

ELKIN MATHEWS AND JOHN LANE, THE BODLEY HEAD VIGO ST. LONDON.

APRIL 15th MDCCCXCIV.

in his care while Oscar was in gaol. Ernest Dowson
died. Years earlier he had fallen in love with an
adolescent Italian waitress in London, and was
permitted by her parents to spend hours in their
restaurant, playing chess, and mooning over the
child. When she reached years of discretion,
Dowson's 'Cynara', heedless of the fact that Ernest
had 'been faithful to her after his fashion', married a
young man of her own class. Dowson's friends, who
had taken the whole affair as something of a
decadent poetic affectation, were amazed when he
plunged himself into a despairing life of drink,
drugs, and dissipation that brought him, broken, to
die in 1900 in a little cottage Robert Sherard kept in
Catford.

Lord Queensberry died. Like Beardsley and
Dowson, he died a Catholic convert. But he spat at
his son Percy from his none-too-penitent deathbed.
Bosie and his brother came to Paris 'in deep mourning
and the highest spirits', as Wilde noted. Bosie passed
on small sums to Oscar from his inheritance: there
was little point in allowing the poor man to fling
away the Queensberry money with reckless
extravagance, as he certainly would have done if
given a lot. Bosie flung it away steadily, with sensible
caution, on a racing stable. But there is no doubt
that he would have supported Wilde for longer had
Wilde lived longer.

Oscar Wilde was preparing to die. As 1900
approached he announced that 'it would be really
more than the English could stand . . . if another
century began and I were still alive'. He explained
his idleness by saying, 'I have written all that I was
to write. I wrote when I did not know life; now that
I do know the meaning of life, I have no more to
write. Life cannot be written, life can only be lived –
I have lived.'

In October 1900, the ear that had been damaged
in prison began to give serious trouble and cause
headaches. An operation was expensive – 'I am dying
beyond my means,' said Wilde – and ineffective.
The doctors said that worry about money was
preventing his recovery. Alfred Douglas
immediately sent a cheque. The doctors said that
drink was hastening his end. Ross and Turner
immediately came over to try and restrain him.
Oscar told them he had dreamed he was dining with
the dead. 'My dear Oscar, you were probably the
life and soul of the party,' quipped Reggie.

By November, Oscar Wilde was dying of
meningitis. He slipped into increasingly long fits of
delirium. Robert Ross sent for a priest, who agreed
that Wilde still knew what was going on and had,
in a lucid moment, signalled a request for Baptism
and Extreme Unction. Two days later the deathbed
convert died.

The Rue des Beaux Arts, Paris: the second
building on the left is the Hotel d'Alsace.
Oscar Wilde died there on 30 November
1900.

left One of Aubrey Beardsley's covers
for *The Yellow Book*. The famous periodical
of the nineties is forever associated with
Beardsley's genius but his connection with it
lasted hardly a year.

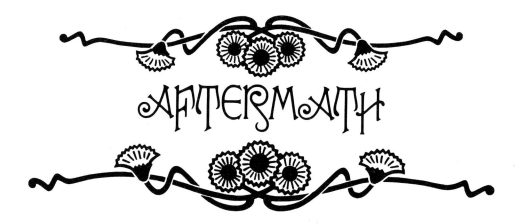

AFTERMATH

'Every great man nowadays has his disciples, and it is usually Judas who writes the biography.'

The lover of beauty died vilely, with an explosive evacuation. Ross cleaned up the room, and was relieved when the body lay, washed and peaceful, after the days of delirium.

The Paris police wanted to remove the body to the morgue when they found that Monsieur Melmoth had been registered at the Hôtel Alsace under an assumed name. With great difficulty, Ross persuaded them not to do so. He stayed in Paris, sorting out the last affairs of Oscar Wilde, and arranging for his funeral and burial in a temporary grave at Bagneux.

Alfred Douglas paid for the funeral, and attended as chief mourner. A few French writers and theatre folk attended; a few English people (apart from the immediate circle) came under assumed names; the two women present were veiled and did not give their names. British press obituaries suggested that Oscar Wilde might well be forgotten now that he was out of the way.

Alfred Douglas returned to a private life which had little hope of ever being anything less than notorious. Robbie Ross, as Wilde's literary executor, dedicated himself to restoring his friend's memory and reputation.

He was helped by a successful German production of *Salome*. When Richard Strauss made the play into an opera, it was confirmation of Wilde's major standing in Germany. A German publisher asked Ross for permission to publish the long prison letter to Douglas which was known to be in his possession, although its exact nature and intended recipient were unknown. Ross agreed to the publication, under the title *De Profundis*, of such extracts as could neither identify nor offend Douglas. An English edition followed swiftly, and Alfred Douglas's review of this showed plainly that he had never read the original, and had no idea that the newly printed reflections from prison were part of an abusive letter addressed to himself. For the first time, a new work by Oscar Wilde received a generally

below Jacob Epstein's sphinx over Oscar Wilde's last resting place at Père-Lachaise in Paris. A monument to Robbie Ross's determination to see his friend buried under a fitting work of art, the tomb was completed in 1909.

right below Salome was produced with success in a German translation, and in 1905 Strauss's opera, based on the play, was not only a musical sensation but proved a lasting success. A moment from the closing scene in the Covent Garden production of 1971; the Salome is the American mezzo-soprano Grace Bumbry.

As the inevitable consequence of a literary life spent in sailing dangerously close to the wind, Frank Harris (left) finds himself being conducted to prison by H.M. tipstaff for contempt of court. A pleasantly scandalous divorce case had tempted Harris's editorial pen to run too far too soon.

favourable press in Britain. The hysterical and histrionic penitence Wilde expressed satisfied his enemies, and the account of prison life was genuinely moving.

Encouraged, Ross proceeded with the project of publishing a uniform edition of Wilde's works. Royalties from Germany and the new book were starting to flow into the bankrupt Wilde's estate, and Ross soon had the satisfaction of paying off the creditors, and accumulating money towards his successful project to have Wilde re-interred at Père-Lachaise cemetery under an artistic monument. A sphinx by Epstein marks Wilde's resting-place today.

Ross also took advantage of an opportunity to make the acquaintance of Oscar's younger son, Vyvyan Holland. He must have been delighted to find that the boy's response to the cold upbringing offered by his Holland-Lloyd and Hope relatives had been to seek shelter in the Church of Rome. Vyvyan was surprised and delighted to meet somebody who esteemed him as his father's son, and was able to introduce him to a cultivated circle wherein the name of Oscar Wilde was loved and respected. Ross was proud to hand over the thriving Wilde estate to its natural heir.

Vyvyan's elder brother Cyril had responded differently to the tragic disruption of his life. He determined to prove by his own vigorous manliness that there was no effeminate taint in the Wilde blood. He began a promising army career, and might have made his mark as a mountaineer or a soldier, had not his self-willed gallantry in the World War led to his early death.

Squabbling broke out among the surviving friends in 1912. Douglas began to resent Ross's building himself a reputation on their friend's name, and he naturally resented Ross's telling all interested enquirers that it had been Bosie's selfish obstinacy that ruined Oscar. When Arthur Ransome published a critical book expressing this opinion, Douglas sued for libel. Ross, who had supplied Ransome with information, now made the full text of *De Profundis* available to him, and Douglas was shocked and horrified to find himself in the witness-box facing the bitter accusations of the dead Wilde. He lost his case, and for some time felt profoundly hostile to the dead friend whose cruel reproof had been brought up against him from the grave. It seems very likely that he had received a copy of the letter in 1897, but only read a page or two of the mighty document before destroying it in disgust, so that he had no idea of the weight and intensity of denunciation Wilde had levelled at him.

In vindictive fury, Douglas allowed an unpleasant associate, the Yorkshire journalist T.W.H. Crosland,

Oscar Wilde as hero. In 1960 two films about his life were shown, one with Robert Morley, who had earned distinction in a play on the same subject *(bottom)*. In the Robert Morley film Ralph Richardson *(bottom right)* played Carson.

right Peter Finch as Oscar. In the Café Royal scene Robbie Ross, played by Emrys Jones, is at the head of the table.

to ghost a book called *Oscar Wilde and Myself,* putting his defence. Crosland was one of those writers who employ blunt coarseness to persuade the public that they are men of sterling honesty, and he had a natural antipathy to Oscar Wilde and everything he stood for. Through him, Douglas roundly asserted that he had never been Wilde's lover, and had known nothing about the homosexual world until introduced to it by Wilde. He also began a vicious campaign against Ross, accusing him of being London's leading pederast, and trying, as his father had done to Wilde, to goad his enemy into starting proceedings for libel. In the end, Ross felt unhappily compelled to take Douglas to court, and history sadly repeated itself as his case broke down in the face of mounting defence evidence that he was leading the life of a practising homosexual. Fortunately matters stopped there, and no further proceedings were taken against him, but the strain affected his health, and he died prematurely in 1918. Douglas had by now become a fervent, if rather narrow, Catholic himself, and he had been outraged by Ross's combination of papistry with pederasty.

Other lives of Wilde were appearing. Sherard had begun his succession of books on his friend, in which he claimed (supposedly on Ross's evidence) that Wilde had died of syphilis, contracted while he was at Oxford. To Sherard, and other naive readers, this seemed to imply that Wilde could not have been homosexual as a young man. Frank Harris, equally incapable of understanding sexual complexities, also contributed to the popular view of Oscar Wilde as a man who 'took up' pederasty in mature life, just as he 'took up' absinthe, or 'experimented' with hashish. Harris lost the fortune he gained by selling the *Saturday Review,* and failed to recover it by various attempts at blackmail and fraud. He wrote a life of Wilde because he needed money and Bernard Shaw, who was sorry for his old editor, lent him the imprimatur of an Afterword. This was a pity, as Harris's undoubtedly useful and informative biography happened to contain huge elements of fiction. Truth was never quite dramatic enough for Frank Harris, and he invented several palpably false 'Confessions' of Oscar Wilde, in which the manly 'Frank' encouraged an uncharacteristically contrite and earnest 'Oscar' to unburden himself. It was a style that paid off, and when Harris chose to write his own sensational confessional autobiography, he devised truly astonishing lovers' conversations to accompany the rich and varied sex-life he bestowed upon himself.

Sherard tried to correct some of Harris's more blatant lies about Wilde but relied too heavily upon his own rather uncertain memory, and he also admitted that he had not been really intimate with Wilde in the early 1890s, the period when Harris knew him best. Alfred Douglas made some reparation in later writings on Wilde, confessing his own brief sexual liaison with him, and trying to write the truth as he saw it. But his animus against Ross remained, and though mellower and more charming than he had once been he was still a biased witness.

The principals in the first great scandal under the Labouchère Amendment were all dead when a new persecution of homosexuals was started in the 1950s. Fortunately, this became so distasteful that it led to some amelioration of the law and, as a side-effect, may have contributed to a growing sympathy for the memory of Oscar Wilde. The early 1960s saw the simultaneous production of two highly sympathetic films, in which an almost faultless Oscar confronted malice and stupidity on all sides. At the same time, the publication of Wilde's collected letters gave the first true and thorough picture of the man.

The bulk of his writing is likely to remain the taste of a minority. *The Importance of Being Earnest* and *The Ballad of Reading Gaol* are equally likely to remain popular and familiar works. And the drama of his life may make him, abidingly, the representative and symbol of a short-lived, exciting cultural movement that somehow proved disappointing in England.

ACKNOWLEDGMENTS

The primary source for any life of Oscar Wilde today is Sir Rupert Hart-Davies's edition of *The Letters of Oscar Wilde*, and I am grateful to Sir Rupert, Granada Publishing Limited, and Harcourt Brace Jovanovich Inc. for permission to quote from the letters and from Sir Rupert's apparatus. *The Letters of Max Beerbohm to Reginald Turner*, also edited by Sir Rupert Hart-Davies is another useful source of Oscariana, and I am indebted to Granada Publishing Limited and the J. B. Lippincott Company for permission to reproduce two extracts from these.

Since Hesketh Pearson's near-standard *Life of Oscar Wilde* was revised in 1954 a considerable amount of rethinking and reinterpretation around the life of Wilde has taken place. H. Montgomery Hyde's edition of the trials transcripts in the Notable Trials series, and his close study of the final period of Wilde's life, *Oscar Wilde: The Aftermath* are key documents. With the kind permission of Mr Montgomery Hyde, Methuen & Co. Ltd, and Farrar, Strauss & Giroux, Inc I have quoted from the latter. Rupert Croft-Cooke's *Bosie* provides an important redressing of the moral balance in favour of Lord Alfred Douglas; his *Feasting with Panthers* supplies a lively and informative account of the homosexual and deviant underworld of the late Victorian period, and his recent life of Oscar Wilde compels some careful rethinking on the use of familiar sources and the re-telling of familiar anecdotes. Whenever I have disregarded Mr Croft-Cooke's caveats against Frank Harris and R. H. Sherard I have been careful to weigh all the evidence at my disposal before recounting some familiar 'incident' whose historicity now seems in question.

Philippe Jullien's lives of Wilde and Montesquiou give a picture of the man and the Aesthetic movement as seen from France which usefully complements Sarah Bernhardt's delightful, if unreliable, memoirs. I have, of course, made the fullest use conscience would permit of the writings of Harris, Sherard and Douglas without whom, it must be added, our sense of the personality of Oscar Wilde would be much weaker.

Of the more distanced biographers of Wilde, I share the general respect for Boris Brasol, and was greatly impressed by Lloyd Lewis and Henry Justin's *Oscar Wilde Discovers America*, a precise and thorough treatment of its subject which seems to me to have received less than its due from later writers. Certainly their responsible documentation enabled me to make several confident utterances, where angels might have feared to tread.

When I began writing, I was without my copy of Lewis Broad's *The Truth about Oscar Wilde*, and quite coincidentally did not re-read a book I remembered as having impressed me until my text was complete. When I did find Mr Broad's work again I was amazed to find how deeply I had accepted his interpretation of Wilde's character, and having just read the more standard literature of Wilde I was able to see how admirably independently Mr Broad had thought out his case, without, moreover, the very substantial help offered by the more recent publications to which I have referred. It was through no conscious act of memory that I not only followed Mr Broad's selection of *hubris* as a key word to the understanding of Wilde's personality, but even used the economy of chapter epigraphs drawn from Wilde's writings to avoid over-burdening the text with lists of epigrams.

Mr Terence de Vere White's life of *The Parents of Oscar Wilde* is more substantial, accurate, and engaging than any of the other works on Speranza and her husband known to me, and I am grateful to the author and Curtis Brown Ltd for permission to quote occasionally from it.

I regret the impossibility of listing the general writers on the 1890s, the actor-managers, café society, and sexual deviance, whose books, borrowed from public libraries on divers occasions for relaxed reading have left various anecdotes imprinted on my mind, and which I have used without conscious plundering.

Dr Sumi Verma gave me expert advice on the psychopatholog of homosexuality and the plausibility of my suggestion that Wilde was bisexual before 1886. Other professional colleagues with whom I discussed Wilde left me regretting that my text was almost complete, and I could not incorporate the critical ideas the had stimulated. The staffs of the library of Michigan State University and the Brotherton Library at Leeds University have been patient and helpful, and Mr Michael Stapleton of The Hamlyn Group has been the most understanding of editors. Mr Robin Seagar guided me through the labyrinth of *fin-de-siècle* Parisian pornography, and made the clear case against Wilde's having any association with it. And my family and friends and colleagues have born patiently with the irritability and egocentricity which I evince when writing.

East Lansing–Leeds, 1972–3

Acknowledgments to illustrations

Colour plates

34 left: Tate Gallery, London. 34 right: Mander & Mitchenson Theatre Collection. 35: Courtesy of the John G. Johnson Collection, Philadelphi 38: Mary Evans Picture Library. 39: On loan to the National Portrait Gallery from the Tate Gallery. 42 top: Mansell Collection. 42 bottom: Tate Gallery, London. 43: Mansell Collection. 46–47: Freer Gallery of Art, Smithsonian Institution, Washington, D.C. 47 right: Mary Evans Picture Library. 114–115 bottom: London Museum. 114: Mary Evans Picture Library. 115: Leighton House, Kensington (Chelsea Borough Council). 118 left: William Morris Gallery, Walthamstow. 118 right: Victoria & Albert Museum. 119: Trustees of the British Museum. 122 left: Victoria & Albert Museum. 122 right: Musée National d'Art Moderne, Paris. 123: Sir John Rothenstein. 126 right: Dr. Conrad Lester. 126 bottom: Louvre (Jeu de Paume). 127 top left: Victoria & Albert Museum. 127 bottom left: Emmerton–Lambert Collection. 127 right: William Morris Gallery, Walthamstow. (*The Aesthetic Movement: Prelude to Art Nouveau*, by Eliz. Aslin, Elek).

Black and white illustrations

Frontispiece: Mansell Collection. 7: Radio Times Hulton Picture Library. 8: Mander & Mitchenson Theatre Collection. 9: Mansell Collection. 10 top: National Library of Ireland, Dublin. 10 bottom: Hodder & Stoughton Ltd. 12: Thames & Hudson Ltd. 13: Irish Tourist Board. 14 top left: National Gallery of Ireland, Dublin. 14 bottom right: Courtesy of the Medical Board, Eye & Ear Hospital, Dublin. 15: Mr. Horace Wyndham, from *The Parents of Oscar Wilde* by Terence de Vere White (Hodder & Stoughton Ltd). 17 top: Irish Tourist Board. 17 bottom: Trinity College, Dublin. 18: Roger Viollet. 19 top left, top right & bottom: Portora Royal School, Enniskillen. 20–21: Mansell Collection. 22 top right: National Gallery of Ireland, Dublin. 22 bottom: Irish Tourist Board. 23 top & bottom: Trinity College, Dublin. 24: Mansell Collection. 25: Mary Evans Picture Library. 26 top left & right: National Portrait Gallery, London. 26 bottom: Mansell Collection 27: J. Allan Cash. 29, 31: Radio Times Hulton Picture Library. 32 top right: Victoria & Albert Museum Library. 33, 36, 37, 40, 44: Mansell Collection. 45: Radio Times Hulton Picture Library. 49: C. J. R. Pope Esq. 41: Mansell Collection. 52 top: Mander & Mitchenson Theatre Collection. 52 bottom, 54–55 top: Radio Times Hulton Picture Library. 54 bottom right, 55 top right: Mansell Collection. 55 bottom: Library of Congress, Washington, D.C. 57 top: Mansell Collection. 57 bottom: Mander & Mitchenson Theatre Collection. 59: Mary Evans Picture Library. 60–61: Mansell Collection. 61 top: British Museum. Reproduced by courtesy of the artist's executors, Sir John and Mr Michael Rothenstein. 61 bottom, 62 top: Mansell Collection. 63: Caisse Nationale des Monuments Historiques, Paris. 64 top: Roger Viollet. 64 bottom: Mansell Collection. 65: Sir Rupert Hart-Davis. (*The Letters of Oscar Wilde*, 1962). 67 top: Mansell Collection. 67 bottom: British Museum, from Lord Alfred Douglas, *Oscar Wilde and Myself* (John Long Ltd., 1914). 68: Radio Times Hulton Picture Library. 69: Mander & Mitchenson

Theatre Collection. 70 top: Mansell Collection. 70 bottom: Roger Viollet. 71 top left: British Museum. Reproduced by courtesy of the artist's executors, Sir John and Mr Michael Rothenstein. 71 top right: S. J. Wingate (*A Catalogue of the Caricatures of Max Beerbohm* by Sir Rupert Hart-Davis. Published by Macmillan Ltd., 1972). 71 bottom left: British Museum. Reproduced by courtesy of the artist's executors, Sir John and Mr Michael Rothenstein. 71 top right, 73: Mansell Collection. 75 top: Radio Times Hulton Picture Library. 75 bottom: Roger Viollet. 76 top: Humanities Research Centre, University of Texas, Austin. 76–77 bottom: Mansell Collection. 77 top, 78 left: Radio Times Hulton Picture Library. 78 top right: Hirmer Verlag. 78 bottom right: Tate Gallery. 79: Mansell Collection (John Arlott). 80–81: Victoria & Albert Museum. 83: J. Mortimer Esq., 84 top: John Kobal (Metro-Goldwyn-Mayer). 84 bottom: National Film Archive. 86: Victoria & Albert Museum. Reproduced by courtesy of the artist's executors, Sir John and Mr Michael Rothenstein. 87: Radio Times Hulton Picture Library. 89: Fitzwilliam Museum, Cambridge. 90 top: British Museum. 90 bottom: National Portrait Gallery. 91 top & centre: Roger Viollet. 91 bottom: Sir Rupert Hart-Davis (*The Letters of Oscar Wilde*, 1962). 92 top: *Punch*. 92 bottom: Mansell Collection. 93 top & bottom: Mander & Mitchenson Theatre Collection. 94: Mary Evans Picture Library. 95 top: Radio Times Hulton Picture Library. 95 bottom: Blake Brown Esq., from *Feasting with Panthers*, by Rupert Croft-Cooke (W.H. Allen & Co.). 96 top & bottom: Mansell Collection. 97: Philippe Jullien. (*A Catalogue of the Caricatures of Max Beerbohm* by Sir Rupert Hart-Davis.

Published by Macmillan Ltd., 1972.). 98: Mary Evans Picture Library. 99: Mansell Collection. 100: From *Oscar Wilde* by Philippe Jullien (Constable & Co. Ltd). 101 top: Mansell Collection. 101 bottom: Mander & Mitchenson Theatre Collection. 102: Roger Viollet. 103 left: Mansell Collection. 103 right: Ashmolean Museum, Oxford. 105 top: Mander & Mitchenson Theatre Collection. 105 bottom: Mansell Collection. 106, 107: Mander & Mitchenson Theatre Collection. 108: National Portrait Gallery, London. 109 top & bottom: Radio Times Hulton Picture Library. 110–111 bottom: Mander & Mitchenson Theatre Collection. 111 top: National Gallery of Ireland, Dublin. 112: *The People*. 113: Radio Times Hulton Picture Library. 117: National Portrait Gallery, London. 120, 121: Radio Times Hulton Picture Library. 124: Arents Collection, New York Public Library. 125: Mansell Collection. 128 top: British Museum. 128 bottom, 129: British Museum. From *The Ballad of Reading Gaol* (Methuen & Co., Ltd). 131: Mansell Collection. 133 top: Roger Viollet. 133 bottom, 134–135 top, 134 bottom: Mansell Collection. 135 top right: Roger Viollet. 135 bottom: Radio Times Hulton Picture Library. 136: Roger Viollet. 137: Mary Evans Picture Library. 138: Mansell Collection. 139 top: Radio Times Hulton Picture Library. 139 bottom: Dominic Photography. 140: Mander & Mitchenson Theatre Collection. 140 bottom right: Mander & Mitchenson Theatre Collection. (Twentieth Century-Fox). 141: Mansell Collection.

The caricatures of Max Beerbohm are reproduced by permission of Mrs Eva Reichmann.

INDEX